SORTING IT OUT

One Disorganized Woman Solves the Problem of Too Much Stuff

---

by
Cynthia Friedlob

THE ALICE JEAN MARK COMPANY
TOLUCA LAKE, CA

Published by:
The Alice Jean Mark Company
10061 Riverside Drive
#165
Toluca Lake, CA 91602

ISBN 978-1-4116-9311-1

Printed in the U.S.A.

Cover art from Big Stock Photo
Cover design by Cynthia Friedlob

For Mom

CONTENTS

The personal stories in this book are fiction, but are based in the spirit of situations that the author is only slightly embarrassed to confirm were all regrettably true.

Also, the contents of some of the *True Confessions* were altered slightly in order to protect the identities of the guilty.

ACKNOWLEDGEMENTS

Thanks to *The Girls*: Michelle, Betty, Jeanne, Wendy and Ellen, for providing invaluable friendship, encouragement and lots of laughs along the way. Thanks to Kay for sharing her stories and for reading every single word of the manuscript in progress, while faithfully cheering me on via email. Thanks to John, the Writer, my generous and supportive other half, for being there. And, of course, extra special thanks to Mom, who will always have the cutest, most organized apartment in town.

EMERGENCY ALERT!

PUBLIC HEALTH WARNING!

WE HAVE TOO MUCH STUFF!

You already know that you have too much stuff or you wouldn't be reading this! And I can guarantee that if you ask a group of your friends, almost all of them will say that they're suffering from the same problem. What is this, some kind of epidemic? <u>Yes!</u> So, let's compare it to an epidemic that everyone understands: the flu.

Just as with the flu, not everyone suffers to the same degree from excess stuff. Each case is different. There are always those few lucky folks who manage to escape totally unharmed. These are the people who want you to "pardon the mess" when you come over to their homes unexpectedly and find the morning paper spread out on the kitchen table and one sock lying on the bedroom floor. We stand in awe of these people.

Sadly, there are also rare occasions when too much stuff, just like a serious case of the flu, literally can be fatal. We've heard the tragic stories of people who were buried under their tons of stuff during an earthquake, or other instances where lives were lost in fires kindled by the massive quantities of stuff that filled a home. Those unfortunate souls had a clinical problem that could have been helped only by professional psychological therapy.

The rest of us fall somewhere in the middle ground. However, unlike a medical epidemic in which there are very easily defined symptoms of the disease, there are few absolute criteria that determine exactly how much stuff is too much stuff. The important issue is how you feel about your stuff. If you feel overwhelmed, if you feel disorganized, if you can't find the time to do the things in life that you really want to do, then you qualify as a Stuff Sufferer.

But don't give up hope! Read on!

STUFF AND THINGS

We are fortunate to live in a country of incredible abundance. The majority of us have more than we need to survive; many of us have much more than that. We may have had to work hard and make some sacrifices, but we're the first to say that the trade-off was worth it. Maybe we wanted our families to have the things we never had when we were growing up, or maybe we were part of the lucky generation whose families were already financially secure and we're carrying on in the same successful way. Whatever the case, we've acquired some nice homes, nice cars, nice wardrobes, and maybe a hobby or two that contribute to what we call "the good life."

But when we acquired all those possessions that we enjoy so much, we didn't stop there. Oh, no. We just kept on acquiring. And acquiring. And acquiring.

First we wanted nice things, then we wanted better things, and then we wanted more things. Sometimes we just wanted new things. But when we got them, many of the things we had intended to replace were just "re-placed." We filled our garages, our basements, our attics.

At last, it dawned on us that we had turned most of our lives over to things. Our friends and family were always happy to give us more things as gifts. Sometimes we inherited things. There were some things that we liked so much that we decided to collect them. Other things just kind of accumulated without us thinking about them. And lots of little things were always needed for our day-to-day life. So, we shopped and furnished and decorated and accessorized and collected and stuffed our rooms and drawers and closets until they were ready to burst. When we ran out of room, we rented storage space. Well, we had to have somewhere to put our things, didn't we?

Once we had them, we needed to care for our things. We had to maintain them, and clean them, and, if they were valuable, insure them. If they were expensive things, we worried about breaking them or losing them. Even if our things didn't seem that expensive when we bought them, sometimes we noticed that we had to start working extra hours to pay for them.

If they were sentimental things, we were always concerned about them. We might even hide them away to keep them safe. After all, they were our most important things.

There were occasions when we didn't quite know what to do with some of our things. But we didn't have the time to deal with them and we couldn't simply part with them, so we decided to set them aside, temporarily, of course. And soon those things started accumulating, too. So we stashed them and stored them and bumped into them or managed somehow to work around them, until one day we noticed that we were positively overrun by things! And if we ever decided to move, Heaven help us, naturally that meant that we had to move all of our things, too.

Then we realized that we had been so wrapped up in the getting and keeping and caring for things that we had lost track of why we had the things in the first place. Certainly, many of us found that we never had the time to enjoy them. Worst of all, when we actually examined all the things that we had acquired, it became obvious that lots of them were totally unnecessary. Just stuff. Clutter. Junk.

Talk about adding insult to injury. Here we were, trading our hard-earned money, our valuable time, our precious lives for things, and most of the things were completely useless to us. That was when we began to think that maybe this was a trade-off that wasn't worth it.

Life is more than things. Life is people and pets and nature and dreams and experiences, too. If we are lucky enough to have the things that we need, life can be an opportunity to learn and love and maybe even to have fun. But, alas, we all have a limited amount of time and energy. We can choose to expend our time and energy on things, or we can use our time and energy to enjoy life.

I've just spent the last several years dealing with my things. What an annoying, emotionally taxing, time consuming experience it has been. And I'm not done yet! As a matter of fact, I've realized, rather to my horror, that I'll never be done. That's because, obviously, there's no way for the average person to avoid "things" completely.

Of course, most of us wouldn't want to live with absolutely no possessions, even if we could. Many things that we own truly enhance our lives or simply give us genuine pleasure. Those possessions have value. But we need to be able to identify which things are valuable and which things aren't. That means that every day of our lives decisions have to be made about things. Every single day. Do we need this thing or do we just want it? Has this thing passed its prime? Should we throw it out or donate it? Is this thing broken? Should we fix it or forget it?

It's amazing how these simple questions can provoke an enormous amount of anxiety. For me, the usual way to deal with that anxiety in the past has been to postpone making a decision. I am living proof that this is the road to ruin. Things start to accumulate faster than wire coat hangers in a crowded closet.

And yet, I do believe that there is hope, even for the most junk-laden, clutter-smothered, stuff-suffocated of us. It takes a whole lot of work, a painful amount of honesty, and a mountain of trash bags, but we all can unburden ourselves and reclaim our lives. Although sorting out all of our stuff and things is a huge undertaking, the results are positively joyous. It's a trade-off of time and energy that I can guarantee is worth it. I have personally experienced the rewards of a bit of empty space here, an organized closet there, even an occasional free weekend on the calendar!

The number of people I've talked to who feel overwhelmed by all of their junk and clutter has amazed me. It's a problem that's much more common than I had suspected. The purpose of this book is partly to encourage others to tackle their stuff and things, and partly to keep myself on track in my own efforts to un-stuff and un-clutter my life. Yes, I'm still down there in the trenches right alongside you. We're in this mess together, but I have faith that we can get out of it! Let me tell you a story about how the light finally dawned on me.

* * * * *

"Of all possessions, a friend is the most precious."

<u>Herodotus</u>
c. 484-424 B.C.

MY STORY: THE BEGINNING OF THE END

"I am in agony," I moaned over the phone to my friend, Madelaine. "Everywhere I look there are enormous stacks of papers. I have magazines from last October that I haven't read yet. I haven't filed anything since the Bush administration – the first one."

"It can't be <u>that</u> bad," she laughed. I heard her furiously tapping on the keyboard of her computer as the faint voice of Oprah chattered in the background. Maddy is one of those multi-tasking types.

"My checkbook is in there somewhere," I sighed.

"That's only a problem if you can't find your credit cards," she responded cheerfully.

Small comfort, I thought, that I probably still could do that. "But this place is completely out of . . ."

"Uh-oh. Gotta run. Boss on the rampage," Maddy hurriedly signed off.

I looked around sadly at the pathetic ruins of what should have been my home office. Newspapers were piled against one wall. Books were leaning precariously at the side of my chair. There were scattered stacks of photographs, and recipes, and amusing cartoons I had clipped to save for those moments when a little levity was the only thing that kept me from crawling back under the covers of my bed. And papers . . .papers were everywhere.

It looked like I had two choices: dive into the morass like a marauding pirate on a quest for my missing checkbook, or head for the local Java Joynt and lose myself in a decaf and a sliver of something chocolate. Only after several moments spent pondering the obvious merits of choice number two did it occur to me that I might actually attempt to get organized.

Organization is a concept that is not totally foreign to me. I used to be organized. Of course, that was way back when I didn't have as many things to occupy my time and energy. And back when I didn't own as much stuff. Through the years I had always maintained good intentions but, alas, postponed any actual efforts to organize until I had the time for it. Of course, no one ever has "the time for it." Now, ages later, the result was inevitable: an overwhelming mess.

This was a particularly distressing situation because I was raised in an organized home. My mother, who deservedly holds the title of World's Most Organized Woman, always kept a sparkling, tidy house. She was never dictatorial about neatness; it was just the natural way the household operated. Now Mom is living on her own in a teensy apartment, and that little place is always bright and orderly, too. I used to think this was due to her exceptional organizing skills and a hefty dose of Protestant work ethic. Eventually I realized the truth: Mom is a genetic anomaly. She's a rare, exotic breed that actually enjoys things like labeling and filing. Regrettably, I fear that most of the rest of us face a slow, inexorable decline into a state of utter chaos.

Confronted with the tragic scenario in my own home, I tried to consider the situation logically. Obviously I didn't inherit the organizing gene. I had to admit that was a definite disadvantage. But it didn't mean the task was insurmountable. I was well educated. I was reasonably intelligent. I had office supplies.

More importantly, I remembered that I had an out-of-town guest coming for dinner very soon. Darlene was an old friend who was zipping through town on a business trip. We had shared all kinds of adventures when we were in school together eons ago and I looked forward to her visit. But she did have one annoying quality. She was perfect. She was always perfectly groomed, perfectly dressed, living in a perfectly charming house and working a perfectly successful and satisfying job. She even had a perfect husband and perfect children. If she hadn't always been a perfectly down-to-earth, nice person, she would have been completely unbearable.

A moment's introspection about my life made me uncomfortably aware that there were some elements, well, perhaps many elements, that might not exactly measure up to Darlene's standards. Clearly there was no way to whip every aspect of my existence into shape before she arrived, but I did think that maybe I could at least get my office together. How fabulous it would be to have something of my own that was perfect! In fact, why not organize the whole house? How hard could it be, if I simply set my mind to it?

Distress over the chaos in front of me quickly gave way to that ancient and powerful motivator, the opportunity to show off. Would I be conquered by the mounds of mail-order catalogs, the treasure trove of outdated reading material, the mysterious piles chock full of things that absolutely needed to be attended to last week or last month or (oh, no!) last year? Impossible! I refused to succumb to the paper monster. But first, could a small decaf and a little morsel of chocolate hurt?

* * * * *

Some people make a decision to change an important aspect of their lives, like starting an exercise program or giving up smoking, and then keep this decision to themselves. It's a private commitment that has strong personal meaning, but doesn't require discussion with others.

I'm not one of those people. As soon as I decide to do something, I blab it around to everyone in the hope that I'll be too embarrassed not to follow through. Unfortunately, that approach usually doesn't work. As a result, I have learned to live fairly comfortably, and fairly regularly, with embarrassment. But I am ever the optimist. So, having decided to get organized, naturally I felt compelled to share.

"I've started a brand new program of total organization!" I announced proudly to my partner-in-life, the Writer. Typically, it was not just a casual comment that I was going to straighten the place up a bit. No, I was already anticipating the perfection that was sure to follow.

"Mmmmmm," he responded. He was staring at his laptop, deep in thought. In these circumstances, he's inclined to mutter and nod affably rather than actually refocus his attention.

"I mean it. I'm starting in my office. I'm going to tackle those piles of paper until they have completely disappeared!" I vowed. "And after I finish organizing it, we can go out to dinner to celebrate."

7

"Sounds good," he replied, eyes still glued the screen. Clearly my exciting new plan had not made a significant impact. Of course, he also had heard me announce a few other grandiose plans that didn't quite come to fruition, so perhaps he harbored a tad bit of skepticism. No matter. I'd just head downstairs and get to work.

"He'll be so impressed when I'm done," I thought happily.

Even the most organizationally impaired person knows that when one is confronted with tons of paper, sorting it is the first step toward making order out of chaos. Sorting was a task that didn't seem to ask much of the sorter. One determines the necessary categories, then assigns each piece of paper to the appropriate one, and, voila! Organization. I had already decided that three categories were required: "Do It," "Do It Now," and "Do It Now – Emergency!!!" I felt confident that they would cover every contingency I could encounter.

I surveyed the unpleasant scene in my office and quickly realized that there were so many piles of paper, all unidentified, that it really didn't matter where I began. So, arbitrarily I lifted one of the imposing stacks from its perch on top of an ancient stereo speaker. Transparent window envelopes were peeking out of the middle, so I assumed there were bills in there somewhere. Even the most organizationally impaired person knows that bills require payment, preferably in a timely fashion. Clearly I should locate those unpaid bills and handle them first. I was quite pleased that I now had not only a definite plan of attack, but also a specific goal. This really wasn't going to be so difficult. Eagerly I began to explore the stack.

"Sweetie, look at this," I called out, a few minutes later. "There's a Fred Astaire/Ginger Rogers film festival tonight and they're showing 'The Band Wagon.' Do you want to see it?"

"Can't. Deadline tomorrow," the Writer called back.

"That's okay. Anyway, it's starting . . . uh . . . right now," I said.

I continued rifling through the stack, noting several more items of interest.

"Oh, no! I forgot to tell you we were invited to the opening of that new gallery downtown," I called up the stairs again.

8

"When is it?" the Writer asked.

"Ummmm . . . two weeks ago."

"Guess we won't go."

"No."

Okay, so a couple of opportunities had been missed. Not important. I forged ahead with the sorting process, interrupting the Writer just often enough that he felt compelled to inform me rather emphatically that a little less sharing would greatly facilitate his creative efforts, thank you very much. I demurred to his wishes for silence and continued, quietly, excavating.

I discovered a recipe for a Mexican Christmas veggie tamale dish that would have been an enjoyable treat had I found it several months prior, during the actual Christmas holidays. There were a few greeting cards from well-wishers on my last birthday . . . and the birthday before that. And there were several applications from various credit card companies explaining the advantages of signing up immediately. "Zero percent interest until 2003!" they all touted. Perhaps I had let this pile of papers languish just a bit too long.

After about an hour of slogging through Stack Number One, I had found no unpaid bills, just ominous, empty window envelopes. But everything else had been neatly sorted into categories. Unfortunately, there were not my originally planned three categories, but seventeen, including one I had decided to call "Do It Later."

"I must rethink this system," I muttered as I paced the floor, carefully avoiding all of the neatly placed mini-stacks. Obviously, bold action needed to be taken.

"Sweetie?" I called up the stairs. "Maybe we should go to dinner now. I'm not sure how long this organizing thing is going to take."

* * * * *

A beautiful, crisp morning had just dawned, as I glided down the stairs from the bedroom and into my home office. I was greeted by amber sunshine streaming through the many pristine windows. A small vase of fresh flowers rested next to my computer, which sat, a solitary beacon, on its luminous white desk. The ample bookcases, filled with the works of my favorite authors, fairly gleamed. The polished filing cabinets beckoned me to pull out my latest writing efforts from their color-coded folders and begin my work. I surveyed my small yet flawlessly organized domain with utter joy and serenity.

Then I woke up. Reality was a whole other animal. It was long past dawn when I stumbled out of bed, literally, tripping over a cardboard box of books that was injudiciously placed nearby. I hopped vigorously on my usable foot and selected an especially eloquent assortment of words to describe my feelings. I had to get those books out of that box and onto a bookshelf sometime soon.

Groggily, I headed into the bathroom for a shower that I knew would put me back in touch with my senses. My faith was rewarded, though my first heightened sensation unfortunately involved more pain. I had tripped again, this time over the clothes rack I had set up to dry one of those ridiculous "dry flat" sweaters. The sweater was draped across the top of the rack in a way that might possibly be described as flat, if one accepted undulating waves of knitted fabric as a part of that description. Why, in this century, anything should require flat drying eluded me. It also eluded me why I ever bought the sweater, knowing that this was going to be part of the maintenance routine. I would contemplate that mystery later.

In the shower, I had to choose from seven bottles of shampoo and five bottles of conditioners, all different. Each one promised miracles. Since I had recently cut my hair rather short, small miracles were all that were required. My first decision was that one really should not be confronted with decisions so early in the morning. I finally selected the shampoo with green tea and the conditioner with crushed walnuts. Perhaps my hair would get a nutritional boost, although why tea and nuts were good for the hair was another mystery to save for later contemplation.

I popped out in mere minutes, refreshed and ready to tackle my day, just as soon as I located my hairdryer. I muttered to myself as I rummaged through all the confusion under the sink, including ancient and malfunctioning hot rollers, four boxes of off-brand tissues that made me sneeze even more when I used them, and several additional bottles of miracle shampoo. No luck.

The top of the bathroom vanity was the very embodiment of its name, with every kind of cream, lotion and make-up that had been invented since I had reached puberty. Apparently the passage of time had been sufficient to allow the beauty industry to create several billion products. The presence of all these appearance-enhancing potions was a bit ironic, since I rarely wore any of them, other than sunscreen and a bit of lip gloss.

I finally discovered the hairdryer hiding under the special towel that dries your hair faster than a regular towel. Some kind of micro-fiber trickery, the saleswoman had said. So far I'd not gotten around to trying it out and I was beginning to feel that the only trickery involved was getting me to buy it. I fluffed my hair the usual way, with heat, and put on the traditional sunscreen and gloss. Then I went all out and added a touch of mascara. I felt positively glamorous.

Pulling my outfit together for the day was easy. I opened my closet and grabbed my standard uniform of black pants and a black sweater. Okay, black sweats and a sweatshirt were the real standard uniform, but today I was meeting Madelaine for brunch and I had to look more presentable to dine in public.

I noticed that the pants were rather badly wrinkled. I speculated that perhaps this was the result of being smashed mercilessly against all the other pants and shirts that I had crammed into the closet. I perused the closet briefly and wondered if it violated some law of physics to have more items packed inside it than the outside dimensions logically allowed. I would need to find a physicist to consult about that someday, I concluded.

Meanwhile, the sweater was in reasonably good shape, though I noticed that it probably should have been stored on a shelf or in a drawer. It was stretched out to a length that made it a perfect fit should I choose this morning to begin using stilts. It also had those little bumps in the shoulders that occur when a garment's weight pulls it down too hard on its hanger. Oh, well. At least I knew the colors matched. I had learned that trick from Madelaine, who often recited the mantra, "Think pink, buy black." It was one bit of wisdom that had truly paid off for me. My wardrobe, at least the clothes I wore most often, was almost exclusively black, so there were no color-clashing problems. Fit and cut were yet to be mastered, but frankly I had enough trouble trying to abide by my own mantra, which was, "Just don't look so awful that you'll embarrass yourself."

Shoes. Where were my shoes? Certainly not in the closet, though there was a decent assortment to choose from on the floor. I should get them all into that hanging shoe rack sometime, I thought. Of course, I'd actually have to hang the hanging shoe rack first. Currently it was stashed on the floor of the closet, awaiting the moment when I would put it to use as something other than a daily obstacle.

Under the bed proved fruitless in the search for footwear, so I charged ahead, down the stairs. I carefully made my way, avoiding any of the many items that might dangerously accelerate my progress, such as the stack of magazines on one step and the bottles of water on another. In a two-storey home, bottles of water seem to get hauled up and down with irritating regularity. I placed the bottles right there on the stairs so that I would remember to carry them with me whenever I made the trip. This system was probably ill advised, however, especially in an earthquake zone. Tumbling and bobbling water bottles undoubtedly would be most unwelcome during a hasty exit. But I chose to ignore that risk, deciding that I would want to be well hydrated, even in a state of total panic. Amazingly, although the bottles were right there in front of me, I still often would forget to carry them up. I finally decided to justify the return trips by acknowledging that they were my only guarantee of aerobic exercise on an average day.

When I reached the bottom of the stairs, I faced my office and gasped. It was such a jarring contrast to the lovely office in my dream. I quickly turned away from the numerous stacks and piles, the scattered computer CDs, the unopened mail.

I hurried into the kitchen to grab a cup of instant decaf for the road. I had given up caffeine years ago, but, psychologically, I still needed to believe that decaf would somehow boost my energy and productivity. This was a fine example of the kind of delusion the human mind is capable of fostering. It was not unlike the delusion I retained that I only needed to lose five pounds. But that's another story.

Every cup in the entire household was in the dishwasher. Were they clean? Possibly. I had purchased a cute little magnetic sign that said "clean" on one side and "dirty" on the other and stuck it on the dishwasher. This was supposed to provide an easy way to keep the situation straight without actually having to remember anything. But remembering to turn the sign around to the correct side was still required and I had found that even that tiny task was often more than I could handle. I pulled out a mug and hastily washed it under the tap.

Coffee at last. The delusion of clear thinking it produced allowed me to spot my missing shoes under a chair in the dining room. On the floor by the chair, I noticed the well-read newspapers of the last several days and a few magazines that contained witty and informative articles that I planned to clip out and preserve, sometime prior to the next millenium. There was also a year's worth of catalogues for various home décor and apparel companies, each of which guaranteed that I'd be rich, attractive, and irresistibly popular if I simply purchased their products. Or so the photographs in them made it seem. Oh! And there was my checkbook!

Finally appropriately shod, fully decaffeinated, and suffering only minor bruises from my morning's activities, I rejoiced that the day had gotten off to a relatively uncomplicated start. Then I headed out the door and down the street to meet Maddy at our regular hangout, Chez Bagel.

* * * * *

Chez Bagel was a pretentious little bistro with an identity crisis. Its menu offered a peculiar range of choices, from New York-style bagels and cheeseburgers with fries to classic croissants and imported pastries. The tables were covered in white linen and there were cheap, slightly ragged old film noir posters on the walls. The fashionably thin waiters wore ultra-tight black pants and equally snug t-shirts with rolled-up sleeves. They all had attitudes. They were Very French.

Madelaine had not yet arrived, so I chose my favorite spot by a window that overlooked the busy street in the front. I tried unsuccessfully to spread out the newspaper I had brought along over the too-small table. Then I felt an ominous presence hovering above me.

"Wooood madam care for zee coffee while she waits?"

I looked up to see the lean figure of Antoine, staring down his disapproving patrician nose. Antoine was one of only three exceedingly hostile employees at Chez Bagel, so he had served us frequently. This is using the term "served" in its broadest possible sense, of course. Usually he tossed the plates on the table while glowering and muttering something undoubtedly unpleasant under his breath.

"Yes. Most kind of you, Antoine," I replied, attempting to unnerve him with equally condescending politeness. He smiled in a way that let me know it hadn't worked, but did see fit to pour some decaf before slithering off. It's amazing what one will tolerate for a decent veggie pate, I thought.

Within moments, Maddy arrived. She bounced in, full of energy, having already taken a morning bike ride and a yoga class. I sighed and silently forgave her.

"What's up? You sounded weird on the phone," she inquired, tossing aside her jacket and barely squeezing into the chair opposite me. The tables at Chez Bagel were always set up so that only one customer, or "klee-awnt" as Antoine insisted on calling them, could sit comfortably. The other chair was inevitably squooshed against a wall or the side of another table. I had always assumed that it was because the place was supposed to resemble a Parisian café where it was fashionable to sit alone, sipping espresso and brooding meaningfully.

"It's this organizing thing. It's a much bigger project than I anticipated," I mused.

"Hmmm. Well, if you're going to get organized, you need organizing supplies," Maddy suggested. "You probably just don't have the right things to control the situation."

"But I've already gone to 'Bed, Office and Hardware' and bought a whole bunch of baskets and crates and containers," I replied. "Did you know that you can even buy containers for your containers?"

"Interesting. Then what do you put those containers in, more containers?" Maddy wondered, only slightly confused.

I ignored her question and continued. "The point is that I've been sorting and stacking and sorting and stacking, but I don't seem to be making much progress. I've been thinking that maybe I should just learn to live in chaos. I could try to adapt. Be more flexible. Maybe chaos is really not so bad."

Maddy pondered this option. "They say the universe is in a state of chaos. Maybe if you're in chaos like the universe, you actually sort of fit in and that would mean you already are organized," she speculated.

I tried desperately to follow the logic of her argument. It hurt my head. "Who says the universe is in chaos?" I asked.

"I don't know for sure. I think some physicists wrote a book about it."

"Physicists? I wish one of them could take a look at my closet…"

"Madams?" Antoine interrupted, offering to allow us the privilege of ordering. It was a crisis situation so we chose to dine accordingly on low-cal fruit plates followed, quite sensibly, by chocolate cheesecake.

We spent the next hour debating the merits of chaos versus organization, both us alternating between the defense and condemnation of each option. The issues were becoming far too complex. There appeared to be no hope for resolution. I began to brood, in appropriate Parisian fashion. How was I to proceed when I felt completely overwhelmed?

My brooding ended abruptly when Maddy accidentally spilled her espresso all over Antoine as he cleared our table. He seethed momentarily, then presented our bill without a word.

As we made a particularly hasty exit, we glanced back to see Antoine gesturing forcefully to his co-workers and speaking his native tongue at a speed that would have been appropriate for a Grand Prix racecar. He paused and the three stylish waiters glared at us. We felt very Not French.

"Maybe we should find another place to meet for awhile," Maddy suggested, shuddering slightly. I agreed that there must be more than one café in town that served both brioche and pigs-in-a-blanket.

* * * * *

"See you next week," I called out to Maddy as I trudged away from Chez Bagel. Next week. The date of Darlene's arrival. I had hoped to have the whole house totally organized by the time she got to town. In my current state of mind, I could barely imagine doing a decent job of tidying up my spice cabinet.

I had tried in vain to sort. I had failed miserably at filing. Preparing some kind of system that would be useful to keep everything organized in the future was a totally incomprehensible task. Yet the disorganization was truly driving me crazy and, even worse, I had to admit that it seemed to pervade every aspect of the house. I was going to tackle my office, but I had come to the painful conclusion that the office was just the tip of the infamous deadly iceberg. In the den, abandoned and unlabelled CDs were stacked haphazardly around a large potted plant. On the overburdened kitchen countertops, unused cookbooks, decorative figurines, and candles vied for space with boxes of tea, expired coupons, and scraps of paper containing notes and telephone messages that at one time seemed worthy of remembering. The bedroom closet was bursting with clothes that had been around since the days when I was a comfortable size seven. Clearly this organizational problem was a full-fledged crisis.

16

"There's just such a gigantic amount of <u>stuff</u>. Stuff everywhere. Too much stuff!" I muttered to myself as I continued on my walk. How did I accumulate so much stuff, especially so much unnecessary stuff? And why was it so hard to part with it, even when I knew it was totally useless? Just thinking about it was enough to provoke a Stuff Attack – that desperate, panicky feeling that takes over when one is futilely grasping for a way to escape from overwhelming clutter. In order to calm myself I took several deep breaths and meditated briefly on the yummy chocolate cheesecake I had just enjoyed.

Sadly, the conversation with Madelaine had not offered as much relief from my dilemma as I had hoped. Although I was interested to learn that even blissfully oblivious Maddy had noticed recently that she was having difficulty figuring out what to do with the huge amount of things that she had managed to pack into her very tiny apartment.

Apparently she had invited a friend to dinner and realized that her hide-a-bed couch was the only place she had available to put all the stuff that was stacked on her dining table. That meant that if they wanted to sit on the couch after dinner, she would have to clear the table and re-stack all the stuff from the couch back on top of it. This had been quite a disconcerting revelation and resulted in a few awkward moments prior to serving dessert.

I walked on past a block of small neighborhood shops. The windows were full of lovely things, flowers, hand-painted furniture, unique little decorative pieces. But they held no charm for me as I pondered my fear that my small corner of the world would be out of control forever.

Then, suddenly, in one of those unexplainable flashes of insight that too rarely grace the human mind, I realized that I might be on to something. Could it be that I had discovered the true source of the problem? Maybe the big issue was not organizing the many tons of stuff, but eliminating it. No stuff; no Stuff Attacks. This idea was positively thrilling to contemplate. Even more exciting was the possibility that organization itself actually might be achievable if there wasn't much left to organize. What a shocking revelation!

I hurried along my way home, slightly dazed, but totally re-energized. I could hardly wait to begin tossing stuff out. I envisioned vast open spaces throughout the house, half-empty closets, and the ability to access my toaster oven. I made a quick detour, stopping at the nearby Sav-A-Buck to buy a dozen boxes of mega-giant trash bags and a fortifying pint of frozen yogurt. My heart was racing from anticipation.

I finally stormed into the house, determined that whatever caught my eye would be the first place where I would face down the Stuff Beast. The entry hall closet was directly in my line of sight. "Ha!" I laughed aloud in my best unstoppable heroine voice. "It all must go!" I yanked opened the door and was confronted immediately by eleven large boxes of unsorted family photographs. I was doomed.

* * * * *

"My great-aunt Rosemary left me this," I reminisced to Madelaine as I examined the delicate floral pattern of a porcelain family heirloom. "I displayed it for a long time in my little china cabinet in the dining room."

Maddy had stopped by to offer support during my extremely valiant, but so far minimally successful, efforts to clear out some of the astoundingly huge quantities of stuff that I had accumulated over the years.

"Too bad it got broken," she said.

I held up a few more shards of what had once been a lovely sugar bowl. Only one piece was large enough for the pattern to be clearly visible. "Quake of '94," I explained. Slowly, I surveyed the turmoil around us. "Actually, the place doesn't look much different right now than it did on that day."

We were seated on the floor of my kitchen, surrounded by the contents of several cabinets, which we had emptied completely so that I could carefully assess the value of each item. This had proved to be unwise. The entire kitchen had stuff spread out on every available surface, including the floor, and it was barely possible to maneuver around it.

18

"At least today everything is standing upright and we aren't sitting in the middle of spilled coffee beans and smushed houseplants," I noted, trying to remain upbeat.

Maddy nursed a glass of wine while I sipped some tea. It was chamomile. I had chosen it for its calming qualities during this exceedingly stressful time of trying to dispose of my possessions. I was stressed anyway. Not only had stuff disposal proven to be a disquieting experience, but it also was Friday night and Darlene was due here for dinner in less than forty-eight hours. The fact that the place looked even worse than it did before I had started my "brand new plan of total organization" was very unsettling. I took a large gulp of calming tea and silently cursed my stupid plan.

Maddy stared at the small pile of porcelain remains. "Um, is there a reason that you're still keeping it?" she asked. "I mean, it isn't going to hold any sugar now."

"I guess not," I sighed. I had to admit that the bowl was clearly a bowl no more. "But it was Aunt Rosemary's. How can I just toss it out? It seems so heartless."

"I suppose the guilt would be a problem. Maybe we can glue it back together," she suggested as she pored over the tiny fragments.

This was a fine idea that I often had considered in the past, but dismissed because the bowl had been so thoroughly demolished. Still, I nurtured a glimmer of hope that the piece could be salvaged enough at least to put it back on display. Maddy insisted that we should give it a try. I appraised her carefully. She had been here for a couple of hours, so it could have been the wine talking. She always had a tendency to believe that anything was possible after a couple of glasses of wine. In spite of some trepidation, I agreed.

The first step was to find the appropriate glue. "I've got some of that extra-super-sticky glue somewhere. You know, it's the kind that let's you lift up a Volkswagen with only one drop. That ought to be perfect," I said, rummaging through a kitchen drawer. The drawer was loaded with small pads of scratch paper (wrinkled), pens (only a few had ink in them), scissors (dull), pocket-sized calendars (for the years 1988 and 1993, unused), and a variety of other items of questionable value. I added the drawer to my mental list of areas that needed to be addressed. I estimated that my list now encompassed every room, every closet, and every drawer in the house.

Undeterred, I continued rummaging until I found a small, dented tube of Ultra-Stik-It underneath a flashlight (no batteries). Amazingly, the tube was not completely dried up.

We approached our re-assembly task diligently, with the care of surgeons. We laid out the sugar bowl fragments in an orderly fashion. We calculated the angle of each side of every little remaining scrap and speculated on the fit as if it were a three-dimensional jigsaw puzzle. We found some tweezers in Maddy's make-up case and began the gluing process.

"In a bad sit-com this would be the time when one of us would get our fingers stuck together with glue," I chuckled.

"How predictable can you get?" Maddy agreed.

An hour and a half later, the pile of little fragments was only slightly reduced but the beginnings of a glued-together sugar bowl were taking shape. It was a sort of odd shape. A shape unlike any sugar bowl we'd ever seen before. Certainly not round.

"This is not being a very successful effort," I commented, understating the obvious.

"No," Maddy replied as she leaned back to view our handiwork. "And it appears that, predictably, I've managed to glue my fingers to the tweezers." She seemed to be entirely unconcerned with her situation. The most recent glass of wine must have provided her with such remarkable poise.

Four hours later we returned from the emergency room. Maddy's hand was bandaged, but, fortunately, the damage had been minimal. In fact, even in her regrettable condition she was quite capable of holding the piece of pizza that accompanied what she had vowed would be her final glass of wine that night.

"You realize that we've spent the entire afternoon and evening in this kitchen and all we have to show for it is stuff spread out everywhere and this poor little blob of antique sugar bowl," I lamented.

"I think we should move on," Maddy decided. "I mean there has to be something here that you can just throw out."

"How about this?" I asked. "It's a broken coffee mug I got on New Year's eve at Disneyland ten years ago." The mug's handle had snapped off, but I had, of course, carefully preserved it.

"Hmmmm," she pondered the damaged souvenir. "We can definitely put this one back together."

I smiled. "I'll get the glue!"

* * * * *

"Your house looks gorgeous," Darlene commented as she munched her salad. "It's just perfect!"

"Oh, too kind, Darlene. But it's all smoke and mirrors," I confessed readily, though I was particularly pleased by the wording of her compliment. "You know how it is when company's coming. One must rise to the occasion no matter how great the sacrifice." I smiled and placed my hand to my forehead in my best suffering damsel gesture.

The house did look nice. Madelaine and I somehow had managed to repack the kitchen cabinets with, unfortunately, the vast majority of the items we had removed from them earlier. I had cleverly concealed the masses of paperwork that usually threaten to engulf my office by stashing them in the various bins and containers designed for this very purpose. The remainder of the house had been "straightened up," i.e. all incriminating evidence of the obvious excess stuff had been stashed away where it couldn't be seen. In fact, the effort involved in achieving this uncluttered appearance was positively Herculean, requiring a follow-up with a lengthy nap before dinner. I still secretly feared that a closet door might burst open suddenly, blasting the assorted contents of its cramped little space all over the room and, worse, all over my unsuspecting guest.

Fortunately, there were no such disasters and we had been able to spend a lovely evening catching up on all the latest news. But, since Darlene was an old and trusted friend, I decided to be honest and tell her the sad truth about my supremely frustrating stuff-related dilemma. She listened attentively and made all the appropriate "Oh, dear" and "How distressing" noises.

21

"So, just because everything is hidden away doesn't mean that it's out of my mind. I mean, it's still driving me crazy because I really haven't dealt with it," I moaned, finally concluding my pathetic lament. I got up to clear away our dinner plates and prepare dessert. "I'm sorry, Darlene. I didn't intend to carry on so. And I'm certain that you can't possibly relate to any of this. I mean, look at you. Everything in your life is so . . . perfect." I finally had to say it out loud.

Darlene followed me into the kitchen. She leaned against the counter and stared out of the window with what I thought was a rather strange expression on her face. I scooped two hearty servings of our favorite ice cream into large bowls and got out the coffee mugs.

Silence.

"Darlene?"

Her lower lip began to tremble and her eyes brimmed with tears. "I can't stand it!" she sniffled. "Everyone thinks I'm perfect, but I'm not! My house is a mess. My office is a disaster. Half the time my kids can't find their toys and my husband can't find his underwear. When I left this morning, I couldn't even find my checkbook!"

I was stunned. How could this be? The most pulled together woman I had ever known was actually suffering from the same problem that I was having? I put a comforting arm around her shoulder and steered her back to the table to sit down.

"I had no idea, Darlene," I said, completely incredulous at her revelations. "How could you, of all people, be disorganized?"

She sniffled again and shrugged her shoulders. "It just seems like there's stuff everywhere. Too much stuff."

Clearly this stuff issue was affecting more people than I ever had suspected. And could it be possible that it was a problem for others like Darlene? Maybe there were lots of poor souls who, on the surface, appeared to be handling their lives with incredible finesse and style but were secretly tortured by their tons of disorganized stuff. My mind fairly boggled at the notion.

We continued our discussion over dessert. The gravity of the topic required a second helping of Double Chocolate Mocha Madness and a small box of tissues for the copious tears that flowed as Darlene recounted her own harrowing struggles. This time it was my turn to make the "Oh, dear" and "How distressing" noises. I could hardly believe that her plight was so similar to mine. I also learned that the Stuff Problem is magnified dramatically when there are children and, just to add another dimension, pets involved. Darlene had tried repeatedly to get organized, but the enormity of the task was simply too much. Also, to her chagrin, her valiant efforts were often misunderstood or even resented by the other family members. The whole situation seemed completely hopeless to her.

Since I was clearly not in a position to give helpful advice, there was little I could offer beyond total empathy. Finally, with both of us feeling exhausted by Darlene's tale of woe, we sipped our coffees and quietly contemplated our respective fates. A clock in the den ominously chimed midnight, though it did sound a bit faint because it was in a closet under a pile of laundry.

I don't know if it was the shock of realizing that the "perfect" Darlene was suffering from the same disorganizational malaise that affected me. Or maybe it was the promise that at last there would be someone to talk to who truly understood Stuff Attacks. It could have been triggered by a mammoth burst of sugar-fueled energy from the enormous quantity of Double Chocolate Mocha Madness that we had ingested. Whatever the case, I suddenly felt radically changed.

"Oh, this is simply too much!" I declared, then forcefully licked the last dollop of ice cream off of my spoon. "Here we are, two capable women who have survived everything from the horrors of 10th grade geometry class to the devastation of broken hearts to the insecurity of freelance jobs, and we're letting a bunch of stuff turn us into whimpering little creatures, willing to live in completely intolerable circumstances! Well, I, for one, refuse to participate!"

Darlene was momentarily taken aback, but my rousing speech clearly had stirred something in her. She dabbed a final tiny tear from her eye and rose from the table, lifting her coffee mug high in the air in front of her. "You are absolutely right!" she announced firmly. "I am not going to live in chaos any longer! I will not pay another late fee on my credit card because I lost the bill!"

"And I won't waste another day trying to find the ironing board!" I said, rising proudly to meet her, eye to eye.

"You lost the ironing board?" she asked, looking quite surprised.

"Well, only a couple of times," I rather sheepishly explained. "I keep moving it around from room to room because I don't have enough closet space and sometimes it gets kind of buried under other stuff and then I thought maybe I'd put it in the garage and I forgot and..."

"Me, too!!!" she interrupted gleefully.

Kindred spirits! We laughed and hugged and happily collapsed back into our chairs. We both knew that we were on the road at last to a simpler, saner, organized way of life. We still didn't know exactly how we would do it, but the battle line definitely had been drawn.

"We can conquer our stuff, Darlene," I stated, without a tiny bit of doubt.

She replied confidently, "Before it conquers us."

* * * * *

TIDBIT: DEFINING STUFF

A definition of "stuff," courtesy of Funk & Wagnall's Dictionary:

Informal (1) Possessions generally, (2) A worthless collection of things.

"Too much stuff" refers to possessions that are unnecessary for our survival or our happiness, rendering them essentially worthless.

It's important to note that "stuff" is not always junk. Anything, no matter how rare, no matter how beautiful, no matter how expensive, can become a part of the problem of too much stuff.

* * * * *

WHY, OH, WHY DO WE DO IT?

Why do we do it? Why do we torture ourselves with too much stuff? Don't we all agree that our lives would be better if we didn't feel so horribly disorganized and utterly swamped with clutter?

Of course we agree. We certainly know that right now we're feeling pretty bad about our lives and, more importantly, ourselves. We wonder why we can't get organized. We complain that we feel overwhelmed. We try to get things under control, but it feels like we're running a race and we can never quite catch up with everyone else. We don't understand why we can't handle what other people seem to handle so well. We know that we should be grateful for all that we have, but instead we feel more like we've been cursed. We're usually frustrated and often embarrassed by our situation, and we're disappointed in ourselves for not fixing it. And yet we continue to live in chaos and feel miserable, with all kinds of stuff packed and stashed, or worse, scattered everywhere. It's a pretty bleak picture. What's wrong with us?

First of all, let's stop being so hard on ourselves. We're not bad people. Our stuff-related problems are not a reflection of a major character flaw or an unforgivable moral lapse. In fact, they're only evidence of some habitual ways of thinking and behaving that don't work.

The truth is that we often have many perfectly fine motives that have led us to our current disastrous, over-stuffed situations. But if, as they say, "The road to Hell is paved with good intentions," then we've definitely been the unwitting day laborers on that sad construction crew.

So what's the problem with our good intentions? It turns out that they are actually wrong thinking in disguise. Human beings are very clever creatures and it's amazing how adept we can be at fooling ourselves into believing that we absolutely must keep all of our stuff.

Much of our wrong thinking is disguised as Noble Sentiments. Let's consider a few common examples. We might like to think of ourselves as Eminently Practical, so we keep things because we think that they might come in handy some day. "This old sweater is getting pretty beat up, but I'll keep it to wear just in case all of my others are at the cleaners."

Or we might believe that we are Thoughtfully Thrifty, so we hang on to stuff because it shouldn't go to waste. "I paid good money for this old sweater, so I'll just stitch up the torn seams and keep it to wear around the house."

We might have Admirable Future Plans for some of our things. "Someday I'm going to cut apart this old sweater and sew it into a charming little pillow sham."

Or, seemingly the most honorable of all, we might have Sentimental Attachment to some of our stuff. "My Aunt Belinda made this old sweater for me. Even though it's completely worn out, I could never part with it."

Some of our wrong thinking has to do with our individual personality traits. This doesn't mean that there's something inherently wrong with those traits, just that they have led us to act in ways that don't work out for us in the long run.

For example, if we are naturally curious and find the world fascinating, we probably read a lot of books and magazines. Then we save the good books and clip out the best magazine articles to share with our friends and family – or more likely, we plan to clip them out but usually don't quite get around to it. Anyway, none of this stuff ever seems to get delivered to those folks, but we hang on to it, waiting for that day, someday, when we'll finally get it into the mail or hand it off. Eventually we find our home is completely overrun with loads of engrossing reading material.

If we're creative, we see the great potential for arts and crafts in all kinds of cast-offs, so, of course, we save them. We're always fully stocked and ready to create our masterpieces, but far too many of the empty egg cartons, the tiny wood chips, the scraps of wrapping paper, and all the other shreds and leftovers just end up left over every room of the house.

If we're generous, sometimes we're too generous, especially with our time. We volunteer and over-commit ourselves and end up with the classic dilemma of too much to do and not enough time to do it. So, even though we feel badly about it, we postpone cleaning out the basement or getting our checkbook in order while we take care of our "more important" obligations. Then we continue to fall farther and farther behind and feel even worse about ourselves.

Sometimes we're highly motivated and we genuinely want to do the best job of getting organized that we can. We plan, we research, we strategize, and then we even purchase lots of organizational tools and supplies. We're so determined, in fact, that we'll settle for nothing less than organizational perfection. Unfortunately, perfection takes far too much time and is pretty much impossible to achieve for imperfect people, which includes all of us mere mortals. And meanwhile the chaos keeps getting worse.

It's perfectly legitimate to share a bit of the blame for our stuff problems with our inescapable consumer culture. The wrong thinking messages it delivers started way back in our childhood. In most of our homes, the family breadwinner, or two, was working hard to improve our lot in life, which truly is a Noble Sentiment. But usually that meant not only improving, but also increasing in number, all of the things around us. Once the basic necessities were met, it seemed quite logical to add the luxuries. How nice it would be to have a fancier and much larger wardrobe. What a good idea to get the up-graded furniture and add lots of appropriate "accessories" for the house. Maybe a bigger house would be even better, with lots more things to fill it up. I'm all for luxuries, but they stop being luxurious when they empty your bank account while they crowd you out of your own home.

Also, for practically every minute of every day since our childhood, we have been bombarded with advertising messages telling us to buy new, buy more, buy, buy, buy. In fact, the whole basis of advertising is to make us feel dissatisfied or insecure about what we have so that we'll buy what's being advertised. Mass media images have continually and very effectively pounded the concepts of "new" and "more" into our brains.

Shopping malls have become gargantuan as the sheer quantity of stuff available to purchase has increased astronomically. By the time we hit adulthood, it gets harder and harder for anyone to sort out "want" from "need."

And, unfortunately, somewhere along the way we lost sight of our original desire, which was simply to live a comfortable life. We went far beyond just wanting comfort. In fact, the very definition of a comfortable life became grotesquely distorted into what we now call a "modern lifestyle," which is jam-packed with much more stuff than we need. It's a lifestyle that requires more work to pay for it, more effort to maintain it and usually no time to enjoy it.

So, the pattern was set from the very beginning of our lives: good, better, more. Things equal success, so the more things, the more success. It's actually quite understandable that we continued our well-conditioned tendencies to follow that familiar but destructive pattern. In fact, we became so good at it that we extended it to all aspects of our lives. We stashed and hoarded everything from pieces of string to exotic perfumes. We saved and collected everything from bottle caps to fine china. We filled and decorated our empty spaces with everything from thrift shop bargains to antique heirlooms. "More" became a goal in itself.

And now here we are, swamped with stuff. We can complain about being manipulated by the media, or blame our situations on the over-indulgent parents who raised us, or the parents who were frugal and taught us to save everything. We can lament our natural tendencies to be sentimental or bemoan the fact that we're always too busy to deal with our stuff. But, let's face it, "oh, poor me" sounds pretty weak when one is complaining about having too much.

Our cunning minds can invent an unlimited number of excuses for the incredible amount of stuff that we've accumulated and feel compelled to keep. Instead, let's all just take a nice, deep breath and confess that not a single one of these excuses is a valid reason for holding on to a whole lot of stuff that we know we should let go.

We can't keep making excuses. Not now, when we are practically exploding out of our homes. Not now, when we are trapped in our clutter and chaos. Certainly not now, when we are facing an emergency that feels like it threatens our sanity. Whatever our reasons, whatever our personalities, whatever our life history or circumstances, we simply must come to grips with the crisis that we're facing.

* * * * *

Okay, so we understand a bit about how we got into this mess. And we acknowledge that we absolutely must deal with this stuff problem and deal with it immediately. Yet we still can't let go. Surely there must be some other more complex reasons why we continue to hang on to so many totally useless things in spite of our better judgment. Why else would we not be living the uncomplicated, uncluttered lives that we say, usually repeatedly, that we want?

As is often the case in life, when one gets right to the heart of the matter, I believe that the answer is a simple one: We just don't want to feel that we've made a mistake when we finally do let the stuff go. The very same nemesis that holds us back and prevents us from facing so many of life's challenges has reared its ugly head: fear.

What if I get rid of it and I need it tomorrow? What if I get rid of it and I find out it was valuable? What if I get rid of it and I feel really sorry that I've done it?

And the answer to all of these fear-induced questions is: What if that <u>does</u> happen? Is your life ruined? Is your health compromised? Have you lost your job over it, or your home, or your spouse? Have you lost your memories of it? Can you think of a single item that you could toss or give away that would cause such dramatic impact? It's unlikely that your drawer full of paper clips and rubber bands could provoke it. Or your closet full of clothes that no longer fit. In fact, your tired-out childhood collection of miniature scuba diving gear probably could go without affecting you substantially. Even if you discovered that some collector would have paid a decent sum of money for it, you'd get over it eventually. It's a truly rare, irreplaceable item that could cause us such pain that we would forever regret losing it. In fact, the special items that we believe have that kind of power inevitably fall into the category of Sentimental Stuff. We'll deal with them later. But for everything else, let's get some perspective right now.

What's the one thing that every single one of us has that truly is valuable? Time. But there are two problems associated with this precious commodity: first, we don't know how much time we ultimately have, and, second, we do know that our time is limited. This is not meant to be a pronouncement of gloom and doom or a prediction that "the end is near." It's just the reality of life that we must remember when we're dealing with our stuff. Time gives us the opportunity to experience life to the fullest, to love and learn and laugh and share. So, let's be clear about what is important. Do you honestly want to waste your time dealing with too much stuff?

* * * * *

TIDBIT: THE PROBLEM WITH "SHOULD"

If there's one characteristic that all of us who hang on to things seem to share, I suspect it's an overdeveloped sense of obligation about our stuff. We "should" find a way to use that old birdcage; maybe we can turn it into a planter. We "should" read all of those back issues of "Tasty Treats" magazine that we haven't had time to go through; there could be some good recipes in there for next year's holiday cookies. We "should" save that dried flower and ostrich feather lampshade from little cousin Eustace; after all, it was a gift and he made it himself. There's no end to the things we feel that we should do when it comes to our stuff.

But if we examine them, it becomes obvious that most of our "shoulds" really are meaningless. We don't have to find a use for everything or keep it all in the hopes that someday we will figure out what to do with it. We don't have to read every word of printed material that crosses our paths. We don't have to keep every gift that we've ever received. When it comes to stuff, there's actually not much that's required of us, except not accumulating so much of it in the future. In fact, I think the only "should" we need to remember is that we should try to live our lives in a meaningful, honorable way, with joy in our hearts. What does stuff have to do with that?

* * * * *

31

TIDBIT: THE PAST

Do you hang on to things from the past because you think they'll let you recapture that time again? They won't. That time is gone.

Do you cling to old stuff because you're afraid that if you lose it, you'll lose the moment in time that it represents? You won't. You'll always have your memories.

* * * * *

TRUE CONFESSIONS: THE DISHES

"My husband, alas, thinks he wants to get rid of stuff but he doesn't. We're currently filling the cupboard space in our newly reconfigured kitchen and dining room and – surprise! – we have less than before. That's fine if we jettison the things we never use, but he won't do that. I got so discouraged the other day that I simply turned away from it and did something else the rest of the afternoon.

Can you use six matching crescent-shaped glass dishes of the kind they used in the '40s when they wanted to serve a salad in a side dish as an accompaniment to a main course? I can't either, but they were his mother's (not that he liked her)."

A Frustrated Friend

* * * * *

GETTING STARTED ON UN-STUFFING

There are quite a few helpful books available about getting organized. They're full of lots of suggestions for easy storage and clever systems for keeping things straight. But these books are really more appropriate to save for a later phase of the process that we're facing. The problem is that their approach usually makes the trashing and unloading of all the superfluous stuff we've accumulated sound easy. The author of what I thought was a particularly unsuccessful volume suggested that it might take as long as one entire week to accomplish the organization of everything. I nearly collapsed from laughter! One week is the equivalent of a nanosecond in the un-stuffing and organizing timeline for most of us. This is going to be a seriously time-consuming job, so we must be prepared to dig in for the long haul.

To get the job going, I do think that it's important to jumpstart everything with an act that is so decisive that you can see some progress right away. This makes you feel good about what you're doing and good about yourself. But it's important to choose the correct thing to tackle. This is not the time to sort through all the boxes of family photographs and finally put them into albums. (Too difficult.) It's not the time to make a decision about what to do with your favorite grandmother's antique hatpin collection. (Too emotional.) I don't even think that trying to balance your horribly jumbled checkbook is a good idea, unless you're having such an emergency that you absolutely need to do this before another minute elapses or you risk a financial catastrophe.

We're looking for bold here, an act that makes a real statement. As always, only you can decide what's appropriate for your situation. It could be rounding up and tossing out every single old catalogue and newspaper and magazine in the place and not worrying that you didn't tear out that funny cartoon to save for Uncle Max. It could be emptying out that disaster area under the sink in the kitchen that's been driving you nuts and trashing the scads of ancient and now probably deadly cleaning supplies. It could be gathering all the bags and boxes of stuff you sorted last Thanksgiving to give to charity and actually giving them away instead of storing them interminably in your garage or the trunk of your car. Whatever you choose, it should be simple, straightforward, and personally satisfying.

Once you make this one big move, clear up this one big task, I can guarantee that you're going to feel fabulous! It will be a wonderful personal triumph and will serve notice to anyone else in your household of your commitment to unload all of your unnecessary stuff. And it definitely will help you get motivated for the hard work to come.

After you've savored your bold act, you can keep that momentum going by tackling the obvious, easiest stuff that you know needs to be addressed. Go for the things that are right out in the open or the stuff that you have to deal with every single day that slows you down and annoys you. Again, choose just one task and attack. Try cleaning off the top of the bathroom vanity and clearing out the medicine chest. Toss all the out-of-date medicines and the make-up that's the wrong shade. Or pull out everything in your jumbled pantry and trash all the stuff that's expired. Then bag all the remaining unopened edible items that you already know your family hates and drive that bag right over to the local food bank.

Once you've taken care of all of the obvious stuff, then move on to things that take a bit more thought, like thinning out your bookcase and taking the books to the library for its used book sale. Or get to work sorting through your linen closet and pulling out the old sheets and towels for donation to the local thrift shop. You might decide to tear through the kitchen cabinets and box up all the dishes and cookware that can go to your younger brother in his new apartment – and deliver that box.

Then, after you're done with these tasks, you can move on to slightly more complex decisions, like what to do with your rickety bedroom furniture or how to handle all those papers in your office.

Think of it as an archaeological dig: every time you clear away one layer of stuff, the next layer becomes clear and you can deal with it. The first trick is not to get distracted. Choose one thing to do and stay focused on it, otherwise you'll start working in one place, carry an item to another place and start working there, and so on. That just leads to the entire house being torn to pieces, something that is guaranteed to make you feel depressed and overwhelmed.

The second trick is to remember that it took you some time to create this unpleasant state of chaos, so it's going to take you some time to get out of it. Don't give up, even when you feel completely fated to fail by the amount of work you face. Remember: it's all just stuff! As long as you keep moving forward, you will get to your goal of a clutter-free, organized environment.

Even if your first steps are small ones, like emptying out the junk in the glove compartment of your car, and then progressing to cleaning out your freezer, bravo for you! The tiniest areas of calm and order are helpful and you have every right to feel proud of yourself!

* * * * *

TIDBIT: PROGRESS

If you really want to appreciate how far you've come after you've un-cluttered and un-stuffed your home, take photographs of every room before you start. You'll be amazed that you ever lived in all of that chaos. So pull out your camera now and get ready to celebrate later!

* * * * *

TIDBIT: WISDOM

"Have nothing in your home that you do not know to be useful or believe to be beautiful."

William Morris
1834-1896

"If I can't use it and it doesn't make my heart sing when I look at it, why would I want it?"

Mom

* * * * *

WHAT TO KEEP, WHAT TO TOSS

I would never, ever presume to judge your stuff. Sometimes we accumulate things and hang onto them for personal reasons that I'm certain would baffle the finest minds in the field of psychiatry. You are the one and only person who can judge the true value of anything you own. That's why the decision about the fate of your stuff rests entirely with you. That's also why you'll get nothing but grief if you try to make the decision for someone else, even your loving spouse or exceptionally well-behaved child. I suspect you'll have quite enough to do dealing with your own things anyway.

Value, of course, has absolutely nothing to do with cost. Often a seemingly insignificant trinket is so loaded with emotional significance that we treasure it far more than any fancy, expensive thing we own. I have a little votive candleholder that I bought for a few dollars many years ago. It's decorated with a tiny painting of a fairytale elf chasing a butterfly. I used it a few times and it quickly got a crack in its glazed finish. Doesn't matter. That elf reminds me of the characters in a picture book I adored when I was a child. So, the little candleholder still sits on my nightstand. Occasionally I use it as a vase and stick a tiny flower bud in it. And I still smile whenever I look at it. That's value.

* * * * *

TIDBIT: STORAGE CONTAINERS

Don't get caught up buying storage containers to organize your stuff until you've tossed out everything that you don't need. All those cute little baskets and decorative boxes and practical plastic bins are so appealing that you can easily get diverted from your main goal: getting rid of all your excess things.

After you've weeded out all the unnecessary stuff and you're ready to organize what's left, that's the time to think about containers. If you can afford it, it's worthwhile to purchase exactly what you need rather than try to improvise with something that doesn't really do the job. Part of the joy of paring down to the essentials in your life is ease of use, so you don't want to compromise on that after all your hard work!

* * * * *

AVOIDING THE TRAPS

After you've made your sweeping grand gesture, it's fairly easy to pick out the most obvious junk in your home. That's the next layer of stuff that can go without any real difficulty. It's the stuff that's headed straight for the trashcan.

A glance through the "junk drawer" (everyone has one) will probably reveal some dried up glue, some dried up rubber bands, and some important reminder notes about opportunities that have probably dried up by now, too. All of that can be trashed easily.

A quick look in the refrigerator will undoubtedly turn up some items that have passed their maturity dates by such a long stretch that they can be considered well into their golden years. We're perfectly glad to throw away those things and feel lucky to have done it before someone in the family accidentally got food poisoning.

A whole factory's-worth of plastic bags from the grocery store that are now stashed away in a kitchen cabinet should signal "too many" without a lot of thought. So it will be easy for most people to gather up those bags and toss them in the trash.

But for some of us, even the simple decision to get rid of those plastic bags is potentially troublesome. It can lead to a perfect example of one of the deadly traps you will need to avoid next. Yes, just because you have resisted the overpowering desire to crawl under the covers of your bed and forget this whole sort-and-toss idea or you have suppressed the frantic urge hire a forklift to empty the entire contents of your house, you're not off the hook yet. There is still plenty of danger ahead.

Trap #1: The Temporary Trap

You are a responsible person so, naturally, you want to make certain that all of the stuff that you're unloading is disposed of properly. Things that can be recycled should be recycled. Things that are suitable to donate should be donated. And things that you know would be useful for or appreciated by friends and family should, of course, be given away to them. Obviously, you have very good intentions. But we already know where those can lead. In this case, they often lead to one of the biggest problems that so many of us face when we're paring down our stuff: a lack of follow through. Without follow through, all the efforts to eliminate unnecessary stuff will be meaningless. And without follow through, you are one hundred percent guaranteed a lot more aggravation.

"Those plastic grocery bags really should be recycled," you observe. True, but you know that the regular trash recycling truck that comes by the house every week doesn't take those kinds of bags. They need to be delivered to that special recycling bin that the neighborhood supermarket has thoughtfully devoted specifically to them. So all the bags get crammed together into one really big bag and set aside, "temporarily," until it's convenient to take them to the store.

Unfortunately, you get so bogged down with other activities (perhaps cheerfully disposing of more stuff) that those bags just sit there, inevitably in the way and still adding to the general household clutter. But since you know that at least something has been done by gathering them up and preparing them to go, you feel that you've been quite responsible. So that's where the activity ends.

Eventually, one day the sight of the bags finally becomes so annoying that they get carried down to the trunk of the car. That's where they sit, and where they're often forgotten about completely, until something very unusual, like cleaning out the trunk, makes them obvious again. Or maybe the awareness that the bags are hidden in the recesses of the trunk will nag and nag continually just below your mind's surface as yet another thing that needs to be handled. But the bags are considered a low priority, so there they will stay, in spite of all that incessant nagging.

Finally, usually in a fit of extreme irritation, the bags are tossed desperately into a regular old trashcan because they have been nothing but an annoyance since they were first gathered up. And you end up feeling frustrated and disappointed because all of your original good intentions have been thwarted.

If this scenario can occur with something as innocuous as a bunch of old plastic grocery bags, and believe me, it can, you can bet with certainty that you'll be facing it again with the more significant stuff.

You finally decide to sort through the old clothes in your closet so that you can donate them. But the bagged clothes end up sitting in the closet, "temporarily," where you occasionally pull out an item to wear because you haven't had time to go to the dry cleaners. Those items then get mixed in with the clothes you decided to keep, so another entire sorting process eventually is required to get out the ones you had planned to donate. Or the bagged clothes get carted around in the trunk of the car for ages (probably next to those annoying plastic bags) until you can get to the thrift shop. Meanwhile, they take up the space that you need every time you go to the grocery store. In some bizarre twist of fate, you might even end up bringing them back inside your home because you genuinely need the room in your car for something else. By the time the old clothes make it over to the charity and get donated, you've put up with some completely avoidable irritation.

You decide to donate a bunch of the kids' old toys, a thoughtful thing to do. So you pack them up in boxes that are set aside, "temporarily," right where you must try to avoid stumbling over them every day. Then the kids decide that a few of those old toys are still fun to play with after all so they pull them out of the boxes. They're quickly bored, however, since these were toys that they already had decided they didn't want, but now the old toys are scattered around the house again. Or, maybe the boxes of toys get stashed in the attic, "temporarily," where they are forgotten or damaged by excessive heat and cold. More frustration.

You pull out the family silver, which you never use, and decide to send it to your sister, who frequently entertains formally. But when you take a look at it you discover that it's slightly tarnished. You decide that you'll polish it first, because that seems only right. So you take it out of its case and set it aside on the kitchen counter, "temporarily," until you have the opportunity to do the job.

But life intervenes, as it always seems to do, and the silver doesn't get polished for several weeks. Meanwhile, it's in your way constantly. You notice that it's becoming more tarnished because, now that it's out of its protective case, it's exposed to the destructive elements in the air. Then the kids accidentally use a few pieces and unknowingly put them in the dishwasher, with very distressing results. More frustration, topped with disappointment for you, the poor soul with good intentions.

How do we avoid this Temporary Trap? No, not by crawling under the covers or calling in that forklift. We must remember that we are confronting a serious stuff crisis and act accordingly.

If your car was about to roll off a cliff with you and all of your newly purchased bags of groceries in it, chances are you wouldn't choose that moment to worry about the unfortunate waste of food. You'd just try to get yourself out of the car before it toppled over the edge.

You are in a comparable situation. Your ton of stuff is about to pull you over the edge. You need clear thinking and sensible prioritizing and you need it now.

The first priority is that you must get all of this stuff out of the house. That means you must watch out for anything that you do "temporarily" with the things that you're trying to eliminate. This intermediate step usually is nothing more than a great opportunity to get bogged down. Following through, all the way, is crucial.

If you're home is overflowing with recyclable bags and papers, the most important thing to do is to get them out of there as quickly as you can. It's great if you can get to the recycling center but, if you need to, this is the time to skip the interim steps of "temporarily" saving and then moving around all of that stuff and get right to the finish line. Trash 'em! You'll recycle again one day, after you've emerged from the current chaos that surrounds you.

If you have items to donate and you can't quickly get them out of the house and over to any place that accepts charitable donations, then use an alternate plan. Pack them in boxes, seal the boxes securely with tape (a very important step), then call the charity and have them picked up on the next available date. There will probably be more than enough stuff to make their trip worthwhile.

If you're going to give away something to someone you know, give it away as soon as you can. The item won't be in really rotten condition, unless you are handing it off specifically to someone who would enjoy fixing it up, so don't worry about it if it's not absolutely flawless. Laundering clothes that will be given to a friend obviously makes sense, but keeping them "temporarily" to sew on all the missing buttons or repair the slightly torn hem probably doesn't. And if you really are sending the family silver to your sister, I have no doubt that she will be so delighted to receive it that she'll gladly take the time to polish it herself.

Remember that the important thing is to get the stuff out of your house. Fast! The primary responsibility that you have right now is saving your sanity. The only way to do that is to clear out everything that is suffocating you and your family. Don't hesitate. Clean out and clear out! All the way out!

Trap #2: The Full Value Trap

Undoubtedly, you are certain that some of the items you've finally decided to part with are worth a lot of money. Well, at least some money. Even your friends agree that your stuff is truly good stuff. So it only makes sense that you should sell it. Why just get rid of things for free when you should be trying to realize their full value? Usually this thinking leads to the decision to have a garage sale. And that, usually, is the wrong decision.

A garage sale is an enormous amount of work. First there are the tasks related to the stuff itself. You already have the huge job of sorting everything, then the garage sale adds on top of that the additional jobs of pricing and labeling each of the items, as well as finding somewhere to store them, "temporarily," of course, until the sale. (The mere consideration of doing anything that's "temporary" should be sending up big red flags right now!)

Then you must take care of getting the necessary permits that just about every local government requires. There's advertising to handle, too, otherwise how will anyone know about your sale? You have to set up your sale somewhere, which may require clearing a place in your garage, which most probably is another big job. Of course, you may just set things up in your driveway or on your lawn and choose to risk the wrath of your neighbors.

On the day of your garage sale, you need to be prepared for "early birds" who will come to check out your wares an hour or two before the advertised sale time just to get a jump on things. That can mean that the doorbell will start ringing at five in the morning.

You'll need to make certain that all of your sellers (family, friends, and other unsuspecting innocents you've managed to rope into service) know which prices are negotiable and which ones aren't. This will avoid bad feelings when Aunt Lucille's butter dish goes for ten cents instead of a dollar. In fact, being comfortable haggling is an important part of the seller's job so you and your helpers can't be shy about it.

You'll also need to be comfortable with plenty of total strangers who will be judging the value of your stuff, unburdened by any of the feelings of attachment or worth that you might have for it. They'll also inevitably want to use your bathroom.

At the end of the day, you'll probably tally up far less profit than you had hoped; there will be some bruised feelings ("Who did that guy think he was, offering us a nickel for my favorite hula dancer table lamp?" "Hey, who put the broken automatic corn butterer out to sell? I was going to fix it."); and, worst of all, you will probably have most of the stuff left because nobody else wanted it either. Now you still have to dispose of it anyway.

Of course, everyone knows someone who had a garage sale that was an enormous success. Lots of money was made and lots of stuff was sold. But it's a fair guess that those people probably were not in your situation. You are in the middle of a major mess. You are overwhelmed and fighting to regain some control over your home and your time. If you are truly in need of the money you think you can raise by having a garage sale, and you think you can handle the additional stress and work involved to make it happen, you might decide to give it a try. But there's a definite trade off. When you are concerned about realizing "full value" for your stuff, remember to consider the full value of your time and energy. Then ask yourself if you really do want to spend that time and energy on a garage sale. And answer honestly!

Trap #3: The Sentimental Trap

This is the deadliest trap of all. Your eyes begin to tear up the moment that sentimental little voice in your head pleads with you to keep everything that has even the tiniest, most remote connection with family, friends, or events that have special meaning for you. For some of us, that can include almost everything we own. But if something really does have sentimental value, how can you simply let it go? That seems terribly insensitive. Shouldn't you treasure it for all your days, then hand it down to your children as the priceless family memento that it is?

Not necessarily. First of all, your children may have a completely different view about what qualifies as a priceless heirloom. Your collection of coffee shop matchbooks from your first cross-country auto trip may be quite important to you, but it might not touch Junior in the same significant way. In fact, even Great Aunt Isobel's costly antique four-poster bed might hold no appeal at all for other family members. Once again, we must remember that just as we can't place a value on other people's stuff, we also can't assume that other people will value our stuff as much as we do. It might turn out that your heirs really don't want every single thing that you intend to leave for them.

As for handling your reluctance to part with those sentimental items that mean so much to you, well, that is a complex issue. I sympathize completely because I have had to overcome some strong sentimental feelings of my own. I found that the only way to get past my reluctance to part with anything I cared about was to remember one fundamental truth: the thing is not the person. Just because someone owned something and handed it down to you, or gave you something as a gift does not mean that you are disloyal or thoughtless or unappreciative of the person if you choose not to keep the thing forever. You are not giving away the love that person had for you, you're merely passing along a token of that love. Your memories and your feelings will always remain with you, even when you let that sentimental token go.

But, understanding that it really is okay to let go doesn't always make the letting go a whole lot easier. That's when it's a good idea to look at the larger picture. We all can agree that we're not going to live forever. Much as we might want to hang around and see what happens next, we're definitely on the clock. Accepting this reality made me start referring to my own efforts to part company with my sentimental stuff as my "pre-estate sale!" I figured that at least if I was the one handling everything, I'd have a fighting chance to make sure that the important stuff ended up in places that I thought were appropriate. For the items that were most difficult for me to part with, that's exactly what happened.

The piano I'd had since childhood had been spending almost all of its time underneath a protective tarp so that it wouldn't get splattered when I was working on my fine art oil paintings. I hadn't even had it tuned for several years. It was time to let it go, but that was a very painful thought. I had so many wonderful memories associated with that piano and remembered so vividly the day my parents gave it to me. But, finally I realized that it simply wasn't fair to have a lovely piano that never got played. It wasn't even fair for the piano, since lack of use would inevitably cause it problems.

So, I searched until I found a piano broker who sounded both knowledgeable and nice on the phone. His criteria for placing a piano in a home sounded almost as stringent as an adoption agency's. When he came over to see the piano in person, he played it so beautifully and was so appreciative of it that it was much easier to let my very special piano go. I confess that I did cry when it was moved out of the house. Soon after, of course, I knew it had been the right decision.

I sold my grandmother's beautiful turned wood rocker on e-Bay. I never thought I would part with that chair because it had been such an important part of my life when I was a child. I had enjoyed living with it in my own home for many years, but I finally concluded that I had been carrying it, and several other pieces of family furniture, for far too long. Our crowded living space needed some breathing room and it was much more important to keep the furniture that actually functioned in our daily lives rather than the pieces that just decorated the house.

Since I knew for certain that the rocker had some financial as well as sentimental value, it was time to auction. To my great joy, it ended up in the home of a young couple in New York, the state where it had been made over a century before. The couple was delighted with their find since they were expecting their first child in a few months and planned to use the rocker in the nursery. I don't believe that things could have turned out any better than that.

Some items require even closer attention to make sure that they go exactly where you want them to go. I had a very pretty sugar and creamer set painted with delicate pink flowers that my grandmother had used daily on her table. It was far too hard for me to sell it, but I already had decided to keep a couple of other sets that had belonged to her.

So, one day a very dear, and surprised, friend of mine back in my hometown received it in the mail along with a letter telling her about it. I already knew that it would work with her china, and fortunately she did like it – or was kind enough to say that she did. I was happy because I felt like I had found it a nice new home where, hopefully, it could become a part of another family's treasures.

One helpful way to ease the letting go of something special is to take a photograph of it. Or, if you're a journal keeper, you might even write a few words about it, the memories attached to it, how you feel about parting with it, maybe even where it has gone. That way you'll have an actual record of the special item, although most likely, once you do let it go, you won't need a reminder of it. If it was truly special, it will be forever burned into your brain.

Also, the act of letting go is surprisingly liberating. In fact, I think that you'll discover that carrying around too much of our past prevents us from living in the present. Great memories and a few special things can be treasured, but life is about change and growth and being alive in the moment. It really would be a shame to miss this wonderful moment of now just because we're preoccupied with things that represent times long past.

TRUE CONFESSIONS: E-MAIL

It took about six weeks for me to write a brief response to the interesting article an artist friend kindly sent to me via e-mail. To explain the delay in responding, I shared the news that I was at work on a book about trying to get rid of "stuff" and get organized.

My inability to act in a timely fashion was a classic example of the curse of Good Intentions. I couldn't respond to her e-mail immediately because I thought it would be nice to write a newsy letter and that would take some time. I was also waiting to see if any interesting art shows were coming up that I could talk about. Then I thought maybe I'd scan a couple of old photos of us that I ran across during the ongoing organizing process, but I lost track of exactly where I put the photos. And on and on.

I really don't feel too badly about the delay, though. It's been over two months since I finally wrote to her and, although I'm sure she has Good Intentions, I haven't heard a word back!

* * * * *

GETTING OVER THE BIGGEST HURDLE

We already know that unloading all the excess baggage that we've been accumulating for years is a huge job. And we already know that we face a pretty big list of obstacles when we finally decide to tackle it. But the biggest obstacle that we must overcome has to be our reluctance to make this job our number one priority. It cannot be something we'll get to "eventually" (never), something we'll do occasionally in our "spare time" (what spare time?) and it definitely can't be something we'll leave for our kids to do when we're long gone (Heaven forbid).

I believe that it's more classic wrong thinking that leads us to resist committing to a serious un-stuffing plan of action. It seems that a lot of us who end up overwhelmed with too much stuff also feel overwhelmed by life. Usually when we get overwhelmed it's because we have allowed ourselves to believe that the needs of other people take priority over our own. The boss demands lots of overtime, the spouse requires attention, the kids are forever in need of something, and we get lost in the background noise of life.

Constantly being available to meet the needs of others, even if those needs are reasonable and worthy, and even if we truly want to fulfill those needs, leads to the feeling that we have no control over our lives. These constant demands on our time and energy can easily spill over to having no control of our homes, either. This results in more chaos, lots of frustration and a pretty poor sense of self worth.

Why do we feel like we're being pulled ten different ways at once? Why can't we do everything we are "supposed" to do? Even if we do set aside time for some things that are important to us, why do we then feel guilty because all the mess and clutter and confusion continue to get worse?

Answer: We feel this way because things really are out of control. It's the only sensible conclusion. We're not inept or scatterbrained or crazy; we are simply dealing with a full-fledged crisis.

So, what can we do to regain our feeling of control and our sense of self worth? This time, we must put <u>our</u> needs first. We must make de-junking, un-cluttering and un-stuffing our lives the most important task we have to do. Every minute we can devote to it, we must. Every bit of support we can muster from our family and friends, no matter how small, we need to muster. Until we clear out the clutter, there will be no relief. And it's not only okay to make this our priority, it's an absolute necessity.

Now obviously most of us can't quit our jobs, hire a nanny to care for the kids, and expect the full-time assistance of our partners-in-life-and-chaos (if we even have a partner). Certain daily survival tasks will continue to be required, but it's amazing how many of those tasks that we think are necessary really aren't. Maybe you don't need to cook so many meals – relying on take-out isn't so bad for awhile. Maybe those committees you serve on will just have to get along without you for now. Maybe someone else will have to pitch in for carpool duty or on laundry day or on that project at the office that requires lots of overtime.

Only you can decide where you can gain the time that you need to deal with your new number one priority. So this is the time to call in the favors owed to you by friends, delegate whenever you can at work, and make your needs known to your family.

Remember that you're not forsaking all your obligations; you're taking care of an obligation that is very important to you. In fact, just to help you deal with your guilt over finally putting your needs at the top of the list, you must understand that getting your home in order actually will benefit everyone you deal with regularly. When you're de-junked, un-stuffed and organized, your entire life will run more smoothly. But most importantly, you will regain a sense of order and stability that will make you a more effective and a much calmer and happier person. You deserve that and so do the important people in your life.

If you can recruit the help of your family, your job will be much easier. A family meeting, or a discussion with your partner or roommate, in which you explain how important it is to you to get your home in order and how much you need their help might result in some real cooperation. You can even try to think of ways to turn the work into something that nets a quick, tangible benefit. Maybe Saturday becomes clean-up day and the reward is pizza and ice cream for dinner that night. Or you might try three Saturdays of cleaning up and then a Saturday of some special activity, like a trip to the beach. Some might call this bribery, but that's such an unpleasant term. Let's just call it a reward system. That sounds so much nicer!

Also, if everyone in the household takes responsibility for clearing out his or her own junk, the process begins to feel like a team effort and the rewards of a cleaned up environment will be that much sweeter when they are shared. As long as you make the tasks manageable, even the youngest child can participate. Picking up toys and putting them away can be just as important as clearing the clutter off the mantle or filing old business papers.

If you can't muster any cooperation on the home front, at least stake out certain areas of the house that are clutter-free zones. If your spouse insists on displaying a large, prized collection of fishing lures, try to agree to confine the collection to one room. If your kids scatter action figures all through the house, reclaim the living room or a portion of it as the adult zone and make sure the kids have a spot that's dedicated to their playtime activities. If your roommate tends to leave the mail tossed all over the kitchen counter, try to agree to put it in a special container used only for that purpose and make sure it's in a convenient place. Every little thing you can do to get things moving in the right direction is worthwhile.

Personally, I think the bedroom may be the most important area to reclaim as a clutter-free zone. If the entire rest of the house looks like it qualifies for disaster relief, you should at least be able to go into your bedroom, close the door, and get a break from the mess you usually tolerate.

If you live alone, there's no one to complain about what you're doing (often a great advantage), but there also may be no one to help you out. However, you might be able to recruit a non-judgmental friend to assist with the un-cluttering. An honest opinion from a trusted outsider can really give you some perspective. The same "reward system" can be used to encourage that help. We must be shameless in our quest for order, even if it means buying dinner.

The first step is yours. Remember: you are completely entitled to declare a state of emergency. The most important thing you have to do is get rid of all your excess stuff and things. It's your number one goal, your only focus, your main activity for every minute you are able devote to it. It's also your key to freedom from the constant torture of too much stuff.

* * * * *

TIDBIT: PROFESSIONAL ORGANIZERS

There's a thriving business community of professional organizers available to help even the most unorganized of us pull ourselves together. However, the first step always requires the "organizee" to get rid of everything that's unnecessary. As we already know, no one but you can make decisions about what's necessary and what isn't. But one of the advantages of having a professional organizer around is that the pro can encourage you to make those decisions. Sometimes we just need to be told by an impartial outsider that, yes, it is okay to give away the electric soup urn you were given as a wedding present but have never used in fifteen years. Yes, it is all right to unload the worn out, old flannel shirts you were saving to cut up and make into a quilt. Yes, it's a fine idea to throw away the forty-seven plastic lids that you've been saving in case you can ever find the containers they're supposed to cover. You don't need to save the forty-seven containers, either, if you do run across them.

For some reason, if we're given permission to un-stuff by a reasonable adult, many of us feel better about doing it. A professional organizer also can help mediate if there are difficulties between partners or family members, though it's unlikely you'll find one who will take on a couple who needs counseling to get through their serious disputes. That's a different kind of professional's area.

A good pro organizer should have lots of ideas for storage options, but more importantly, the pro should have the ability to visualize your living space in a new way. Otherwise, you'll just end up with a neater space that still doesn't really work for you.

TAKING A NEW KIND OF INVENTORY

How would you feel if someone asked you to take an inventory of your home? What would you do if you needed to make not just a cursory list of the big objects like the bed, the television, and the couch, but a complete, detailed inventory of absolutely everything in the entire place, right down to the last thumbtack and half-empty tube of lipstick? It's a pretty daunting thought, isn't it?

Usually the only time anyone ever thinks about an inventory of his or her stuff is if it's been stolen or lost in some catastrophe like a fire. Insurance adjusters frequently comment that one of the problems in making claims under those trying circumstances is that most people have only the vaguest notion of what all that stuff was that they were living with every day. Maybe most of it is forgotten because most of it was forgettable.

But there is a more useful kind of inventory that all of us could take right now. It's an inventory of what we need instead of what we own. If you walk through, or even just think about, each room in your home, I'm certain that you can come up with a fairly complete list of every item that you either use or appreciate regularly in that room. You don't have to restrict yourself to strictly functional items in this inventory. For example, I think art can be considered a necessity and maybe you'd agree. So, if you have a favorite piece of art or a decorative item that you thoroughly enjoy, it makes sense to include that on your list.

What this process offers is an opportunity to understand, maybe for the first time ever, specifically what stuff makes your home livable and what makes you comfortable. My bet is that it's far less than what you have.

Making this list is not the time to pause and seriously mull over all that you own. You certainly don't want to write down every single thing that you see – you already know you see too much. And when you're facing all of that extra stuff, you don't want to get depressed or overwhelmed. This inventory is devoted only to what you honestly think you need and enjoy, nothing more. Your list should be fairly short because it will contain only the big, important

53

items. It can have some pretty broad categories and it will still be quite useful. Making this list is only an exercise to get you thinking in a different way, so don't panic.

Let's try an example. In your living room, you might decide that you need a couch; a chair; two end tables; three lamps; a television and its stand; a DVD player, a stereo system, and a videogame player, along with your family's favorite DVDs, CDs, and games; and a screen and tools for your fireplace. You might really enjoy the picture that hangs above the fireplace, so you add that to your list, too. Remember, this list is the absolute minimum number of items that will make the room comfortable and that will serve your needs.

When you actually look around your living room what you might see are all the items on your list plus:

Three extra chairs for company that comes to the parties you have during the holidays, with throws tossed across the backs of each and two small embroidered pillows per chair ("Bless Our Mess," "Girls Just Want to Have Fun," "Merry Christmas" – didn't get around to putting that one away – etc.); four stuffed animals belonging to your youngest also rest on one chair.

A large coffee table with two years' worth of old magazines and six days' worth of newspapers on it, along with several candles, a vase (chipped), a potted plant (dead), four porcelain ballet dancer figurines, the dog's collar, some unsorted mail, your spouse's mug of hot chocolate from last night (empty), two pens (one has ink) – plus one sock, (underneath said table).

Two artificial ficus trees in the corners of the room (fronds spill over into two of the guest chairs), with an up-light on the floor below each (one bulb burnt out).

Next to the couch, on the floor, a stack of thirty-seven unlabelled videotapes you intend to dispose of someday (they're no longer watchable because you've traded in the VCR for a DVD, but you keep wondering if there's something really good on one of them), another stack of magazines (about fifteen total, various titles), and three of the throw pillows that are usually on the couch (with the other five, but you had to move these in order to sit down).

On the end tables, a portable phone (battery dead from not being put back in its cradle for about a week), your oldest kid's math homework assignment from last Tuesday (C+), the shirts that need buttons sewn on, the sewing kit (no buttons), four more ballet dancers, a stack of the last two years' worth of catalogs from all of your favorite mail order companies, three framed family photos, a wicker basket containing another plant (wilting) and its attendant little plastic gnome holding a sign that says, "Especially for You."

On top of the TV, the last few weeks of television guides, two paperback books, and one library book (overdue); stacked on the floor next to the TV, thirty-four more books, some yours, some belonging to your sister-in-law (and several more, unbeknownst to you, also belonging to the library).

On the mantle (partially obscuring the picture you like above it), eleven more ballet dancer figurines, two candlesticks, a large ceramic dish from your trip to Mexico, your kid's math homework from last month (C-), six more framed family photos, a pot of trailing ivy (trailing a bit too much), the remote control (under the homework), and three business cards of possible contacts from your last business trip (you'd been wondering where you put those cards).

On the floor next to the fireplace, a pile of CDs, DVDs and videogames (definitely not all favorites); the work papers your spouse needs to go through before the big meeting next week; and a handful of your kids' action figures.

On the walls, five more pictures, two sconces and a mirror.

Now take several deep breaths and remain calm. Obviously, there are some superfluous items in your living room. You might even see many, many more than this exercise has suggested. They may be inexpensive little tchotchkes or outrageously priced crystal and silver collectibles. It doesn't matter. The important thing to do now is figure out if anything else that you see belongs on your list. Do you need or love any of it?

You may find that much of what's left belongs in another part of the house, or you might boldly decide that it's almost all completely expendable. You may find that you need to rearrange things so that some items can stay in the living room more comfortably. Let's try to continue the exercise:

The stuff that can be trashed immediately is easy to spot, like the old catalogs, newspapers, magazines and dead plants. The stuff that belongs elsewhere is pretty clear, too, like the mug, the sock, the phone, the business cards, etc. These are the things to address first when you're ready for action.

The rest of the stuff may require some thought. Isn't it time that you got rid of those old videotapes? Of course, it is. That chipped vase really irritates you, so maybe you can toss it, too. What if you unloaded the extra chairs and bought a bookcase? It would give those books a home and maybe all of the figurines could be displayed on one shelf. But do you really want all of those books? And do you discover that you no longer even like the figurines? That mantle looks too crowded . . .

You get the idea. Keep looking and thinking until you've made a decision about everything in the room. For example, if you decide that you really love every single pillow in there because they look so comfy, they may deserve to stay. If you wonder what in the world you're doing with all those pillows, it's time to let them go. If you can't make up your mind about the pillows, try packing some away in a box to see if you like living without them. Put the box (clearly labeled and sealed) in a holding area like your basement or garage, but don't let it stay there forever! If you determine that you like the living room without them, don't even unpack that box. Get it out of your house the minute you make that decision.

If you use this process as a guideline while you're working on eliminating all of your excess stuff, then every time you are considering keeping an item that doesn't appear on your list, you can try to figure out why. Is it guilt? Is it the possibility of usefulness at some future date? Is it because you think it enhances your social status? Whatever the reason might be, once you can honestly identify why you want to keep it, then you can decide if the reason is sufficient.

You can actually add the items you decide to keep to your list if you want to be really efficient about this. Sometimes just the act of writing it down will make you re-evaluate how you feel about an item. But don't obsess over the writing down of additional items. The idea is to get you thinking about that short list of the minimum amount of stuff that you need. Then every time you want to keep something else, at least you'll be able to compare its merits to the really important items on your list of basic necessities. We already know that you're the only one who can make the final decision when it comes to your personal stuff.

If you're taking an inventory of the common areas of your home, including your partner and even your kids in the process is important. In fact, if you can encourage all of the members of your household to make their own lists for their own rooms or areas, it will help everyone in the general effort to eliminate extra things. Of course you will need to help the younger kids, but this will work only if you don't make any editorial comments. Kids can be very insightful when it comes to understanding what's necessary and what isn't, even without any help from you.

You don't have to tackle the whole house all at once – in fact, I don't recommend it. You'll probably end up hyperventilating and have to go out to buy chocolates. Try this technique in one room just as an experiment. See if it helps you get a new perspective. Depending on how detailed you want to be, it's a job that will require some time and will provoke some thought, as well. But when you're done, I think you'll find it has been very helpful in helping you understand how you relate to your stuff. And, whether you pare down to exactly what's on your list, or you add some things to it, you'll undoubtedly have a new appreciation for what you do keep. You'll also have a good reminder of what's important when you're considering buying something new.

* * * * *

TRUE CONFESSIONS: KEEPING THINGS YOU HATE

It turns out that there are some things that you don't even like, but you feel obligated to hold on to them because they were given to you by a friend or relative or, even more difficult, inherited from one. The guilt engendered by getting rid of this kind of stuff is in a class of its own. I have one such burdened friend who recently told me her frustrating tale.

Doreen and her husband had just hauled a half-dozen large paintings up to their attic, the latest storage spot for them after years of being carted around from place to place. The paintings had been done by her husband's late and lamentably untalented aunt, but, even though he hated them, he just couldn't part with them.

The paintings are absolutely the worst kind of stuff to let go: hand-made family heirlooms. It's a double whammy. Not simply owned by, but actually created by the Untalented Aunt. Had they been even remotely appealing, they might have been foisted onto some other unexplainably pleased family member – a trick I recommend highly! But since they are the husband's things, my frustrated friend really has no recourse. The husband is the one who feels the need to keep them and, unfortunately, it has to be his call. So much for the partnership of marriage.

Doreen might get lucky if there's a small leak in the roof during a rainy winter. "Oh, what a shame. Untalented Aunt's paintings have been ruined. We'll just have to chuck them." Otherwise, she'll have to wait and hope that her husband has an epiphany about getting rid of stuff.

* * * * *

TIDBIT: A STUFF PICK-ME-UP

Do you ever buy something to make yourself feel better? We all do it occasionally. But many of us routinely turn to acquiring new stuff in order to get relief from some problem or situation that's bothering us. If we're feeling down or anxious, we'll buy a new pair of shoes, or a new power tool, or another little decorative thing to add to our constantly growing collection of little decorative things.

We know that it's just a temporary fix. We feel better briefly, but it doesn't address whatever the problem is. And buying more things just adds to the distressing reality that we already have too many things. Then we have even more work to do because we need to try to find a place for the new stuff in our over-packed homes. If we can't, we have to store it or hand it off to someone else or trash it.

Kind of a waste of time, energy, and money, isn't it?

* * * * *

TIDBIT: REALLY GOOD STUFF

The concept of saving something because it's "too good to use" unfortunately is very common. Of course, we all have items that we use only on special occasions or for holidays – the serving dish that's only on the table at Thanksgiving, the fancy dress worn only for special evenings out on the town, the bubble bath saved for days that call for extra pampering. But if you have, for example, a lovely set of crystal goblets, fancy china and sterling silver flatware and they're never out of the cabinet, what good are they? If the beautiful sweater Uncle Marty gave you for your birthday never gets worn, what use is it? If the living room is furnished with an ultra-luxurious couch and you hustle everyone into the den so they won't sit on it, what's the point?

It's like buying a new car and never driving it because it's too good to put on the road. If you're not using a useful item, there's no point in having it. Maybe you don't use it because it doesn't work for you for some reason – you're just not interested in setting a formal dining table, the sweater is too flashy for your taste, the couch was simply a really expensive mistake. Well, then, unload it. Sell or pass those things along to someone who will appreciate them. Otherwise, break out the good stuff and enjoy the bounty!

* * * * *

STUFF AND IDENTITY

I live in Los Angeles, the capital of superficiality. There are few people anywhere who can even approach many an Angeleno's obsession with appearances. The term "appearance" doesn't apply only to physical attributes; it also includes clothing, jewelry, cars, and home and office furnishings. It only follows that for those who subscribe to this outlook on life, the ownership of things, specifically the "right" things, is a crucial part of their identity.

Of course, even outside of L.A., every one of us who can afford to shop is seduced regularly into purchasing things that promise to make us younger, smarter, hipper, or whatever other attribute we may find desirable. That's what advertising is all about: luring potential buyers with claims that appeal to our sense of who we are or who we aspire to be. Even something as mundane as dishwashing liquid isn't sold just on the basis of its ability to get your dishes clean; it also keeps your hands soft, or is safe for the environment, or improves your mood because of the way it smells. The way it's packaged influences us, too. We make our choices of what to buy through the studied manipulation of all kinds of complex factors that determine how we feel about ourselves. Logic usually has absolutely nothing to do with it.

Luxury items are the most heavily reliant on image as a sales tool. No one really needs the most expensive car or jewelry or clothing that's made, but if you can be convinced to buy it because it will enhance your status, your love life, or, most importantly, your feelings of self worth, then the advertisers have done their job well.

With this in mind, it should be obvious that it's very flawed thinking to conclude that the possession of certain things also means that the person possessing them is necessarily a superior being. Yet I always find it surprising how many people still haven't figured out this most basic of facts: the truly valuable part of who you are is not determined by what you look like or what you own.

A quick perusal of any gossipy magazine will offer harrowing tales of attractive, famous, "successful" people who appear to have everything, yet they've gone through multiple divorces, multiple trips in and out of detox, and seem to be fairly miserable creatures. A glance at the headlines will reveal others who are wealthy beyond imagining for most of us, yet they lie and cheat and steal to get even more. The rich and famous may have opulent lifestyles, but clearly they don't always have contented lives.

And yet how often are we caught up in buying the latest fashions or newest gadgets in order to make ourselves feel that we're part of a special group of people who are somehow worthier in our minds?

During your sorting out process, if you discover that you're swamped with a ton of stuff that is in your life only to make you feel okay about yourself, maybe it's time you gave yourself a break. If you're a person of kindness, integrity and honesty, you're just fine, even if you don't own this year's hot car or high-end designer appliances.

Once you can get a little separation between your stuff and how you feel about yourself, you'll be a lot happier. And then it will be a lot easier for you to separate your stuff from your life.

* * * * *

IS IT VALUABLE?

Not everything that you think is valuable is actually valuable. Still, most of us cling to the belief that we've got something special that's worth a mint stashed amongst our vast array of stuff and things. It's an unfortunate fact of life that we're usually wrong. Of course, no one wants to learn that the "priceless Ming vase" found at a flea market really does have a price: about five dollars. And it is too bad to discover that the painting you uncovered in the cellar of cousin Jasper's farmhouse wasn't painted by an obscure American old master, but by cousin Jasper.

But let's forget about the hidden gems that we hope will provide vast riches for our fantasy lives. What about all that regular stuff we have? It seems like that ought to be worth at least something. Well, we're often wrong about that, too. In fact, some things may be totally worthless.

For many of us it's hard to admit that sometimes stuff is just old and worn out. If you get caught up in the Frugal Trap, you could easily end up trying to salvage something that would be cheaper simply to replace. For example, not every piece of furniture is worthy of repair. Repair takes time, which is something you're already short on, as well as effort and often some expertise. After you look it over carefully, you might find that your battered old kitchen table might be put to much better use as firewood.

Sometimes a brand new item simply does the job a lot better than an old one. It could be smaller, lighter, faster, have more functions, or even be safer. Would you trade your snappy new gas oven for a woodstove? Or your big refrigerator for a small, old-fashioned ice box? Well, it might work out fine if you were enjoying a rustic life in the hill country, but for the average city dweller the choice is obvious. Many appliances and tools have a limited life. It's not a bad idea to trade that forty-year-old steam iron that spits rusty water on your lace tablecloth for a nice new iron that weighs pounds less and works much better.

It's hard to believe how quickly lots of technology loses its value, too, because it's outdated by newer and snazzier versions. Try selling an old, slow, dial-up computer modem or a giant-sized, early generation cellular phone and you'll be hard-pressed to find an interested buyer. In fact, if you're thinking of simply donating your used computer equipment, it's a good idea to check with the charity first because you'll probably find that they have some restrictions on what they can accept.

Recently a friend of mine thought that she would unload the old "Teach Yourself French" and other language learning records that she inherited. It only took a few phone calls to find out that there wasn't a single place in town that wanted them, including charities and a music library. How many people have a turntable now? The records were completely obsolete.

I suppose it could be argued that there's probably a collector out there for almost every item ever manufactured in the history of the entire world. But unless you want to spend your time tracking down that collector (see the chapter about auctions), you might just want to get comfortable tossing out a whole bunch of your stuff.

The disposable society that we live in now is particularly difficult to accept for those of us raised in an era when things were expected to keep their value for a fairly long stretch and hold up well with perhaps only a few minor repairs. I definitely do my share of worrying about the impact of the new disposability of things on our environment, as well as its effect on our cultural attitudes about value and the level of quality and durability we will accept from the manufacturers of items that we need.

But holding onto broken or obsolete or useless things doesn't help the world's situation or our own personal cluttered situations one bit. Better to get rid of the useless stuff that plagues us and then use our less burdened brains to try to figure out solutions to these kinds of complex problems.

* * * * *

TIDBIT: CHARITABLE DONATIONS

When you're ready to donate your stuff, make sure it's worth donating. Charities have some basic guidelines that we need to follow, otherwise our stuff just causes problems for them after it's already caused more than enough problems for us.

First of all, wash or dry clean all clothing before you give it away. Also test electrical equipment and battery operated items to be certain that they work. If you're donating kids' toys and games, make sure that they are still in working order and have all their parts. If not, just toss them out.

Safety concerns are another major factor that charities must consider. Some items such as cribs and car seats can't be accepted due to U.S. Consumer Product Safety Commission regulations. If an item has been recalled or banned in this country, just put it in the trash. That's what the charity would have to do with it.

Definitely call the charity before you try to donate these items:

Major appliances and large furniture

Computers, monitors, and computer peripherals

Cars (donating can be a great way to get rid of an old junker)

And if you are still hanging onto one of those old cellular phones, check with your favorite charity or try Goodwill Industries. Many Goodwill locations will recycle older models but they also have a new program in some areas that will take smaller, digital models under two years old for resale.

You can get more detailed information about donating on some charities' web-sites. Follow the charity's guidelines and your good deed really will be a good deed.

* * * * *

TIDBIT: AUCTIONS AND CONSIGNMENT

If you really do own some valuable items, or have a legitimate reason to suspect that you might have valuable collectibles among your antiques or vintage stuff, you might consider either auctioning or consigning those items.

There are a couple of ways to go about auctioning, although many people now automatically seem to think of on-line auctioning. The appeal is that it's efficient, inexpensive and you have the benefit of a vast, worldwide audience of potential buyers. I can speak from personal experience that it is a relatively painless process, especially if you're only offering a few things at a time and you already know their value. You are also responsible for packing and shipping the items that sell, or paying a service to do it for you, so that means that if you have a lot of items in auctions all going on at once, it can get a bit time consuming. However, I've even sold large pieces of antique furniture in on-line auctions, so I know that most any kind of shipping can be handled with a little bit of effort. Also, if you're looking for a buyer for very specialized collectible things but there are only a small number of people who are interested in that particular category of collectibles, on-line auctions can't be beat.

Another option is using an auction house to sell your valuable pieces. Again, my experience with auction house selling has been positive, though you'll be giving up a hefty percentage of the sale price for their services. There are minimum values that must be met before a major auction house will want to handle your things. Check with them to see what the appraisal procedure is for the type of items you want to sell. Smaller, local auctions are usually much more flexible about what they will accept, though the price that you'll get for your items may reflect their more limited audience.

If you're selling an item on your own, you'll want to have a good idea of its value. You can find an appraiser through one of the professional associations for the trade, such as the American Society of Appraisers, the International Society of Appraisers, and the National Association of Jewelry Appraisers. Some auction houses have occasional free days in which the public can bring in an item to get it valued at no charge. Inexpensive on-line services are available, too, but it's a good idea to inquire about the qualifications of their appraisers. There's also quite a lot of helpful information available in books or on the Internet that you can track down independently to get an idea of the value of many popular auctionable items.

You also could give some of your special pieces to an antiques dealer in your area that accepts consignments. A reputable, qualified dealer will be able to give you a good idea of the value of a piece and will know if there's a local market for it as well. The percentage varies that dealers take for their services, but I have found it to be less than the commission charged by an auction house. I have sold many items through consignment shops and have been very happy with the results. It's been particularly helpful in selling the type of mid-value, smaller pieces that people often want to handle in person before buying, such as vintage jewelry or crystal and china. Taking a whole bunch of things into a consignment shop is also a great way to get them out of your house quickly!

Finally, you might want to check out local publications that list antiques dealers and collectors in your area who are willing to buy things outright. If you simply want to unload some valuable items in a hurry and you don't want to wait for payment from a consignment shop, this may be the solution to your problem.

However you dispose of your valuables, don't waste time agonizing over whether or not you got the best price for them. Be content knowing that you've passed along your treasures to others who will enjoy owning them and, most importantly, rejoice because you've un-stuffed your home!

* * * * *

One warning: If you take your things to a consignment shop or attend the auction of your items, be careful that you don't end up coming home with more stuff than you had in the first place. The selection of items for sale is usually fascinating and the temptation is huge to pick up some bargains. Stay strong!

"A good name is better than riches."

Cervantes (Miguel de Cervantes Saavedra)
1547-1616
Don Quixote

GETTING STUCK, GETTING UNSTUCK

If you start your un-cluttering, un-stuffing efforts and run out of steam or face more of a mess than you started with, see if you need to deal with some of these issues:

Set specific, manageable priorities:

Sometimes Stuff Sufferers have difficulty prioritizing what needs to be done and determining what reasonably can be accomplished. We need to come up with a list of specific tasks, not just a general idea that we've got to get everything organized. Ideally, each task should be small enough that it can be accomplished in one day, even if you're interrupted by phone calls or car pool duty or an emergency load of laundry. If you're going to tackle a project in the evening after a day at the office, the task that you select must be even smaller.

Take some time to break down what needs to be done in only one area, maybe the kitchen for example, if that's the room that's causing you the most grief. Even though some of us don't like the idea of having to write things down, if you've run into trouble, this really is a good time to make a list.

You might have only a few items on your list, such as cleaning all the decorative stuff and extra appliances off the counters, reorganizing the cabinets and getting rid of extra dishes, and cleaning out under the sink. Start with one of those items and go to it until it's finished. Don't get sidetracked by anything else. Don't worry that the living room needs attention, too, or that the den is under a sea of business papers. Stay focused until you're done.

After you've completed that task, don't start another one unless you can be reasonably certain that you can finish it in the same day. If you can't, you can either call it a day and celebrate what you've accomplished – in fact, you should <u>always</u> celebrate what you've accomplished! – or you can find a smaller task that you also can complete before your day's over.

Let's say that you get the area under the sink cleaned out and all the trash taken out to your trash can. If you're short on time, you might break down the job of dealing with the countertops into a couple of smaller tasks. Maybe you decide to move or store or dispose of all the decorative stuff. You can save dealing with the appliances for another day because you know that task will require a big effort to find room for them somewhere inside your crowded cabinets. If you don't wait for another day, you risk having half of the stuff inside your cabinets spread out all over your kitchen. Then, just as you're trying to figure out what you're going to do with all of it, suddenly it's midnight. Remember: the task has to be manageable in the time period that you have available to do it.

Embrace change and the future:

Even though we are unhappy with the way things are, we often have a tendency to cling to the familiar. Usually that's because we have not yet formed a clear picture in our minds about what our changed life will be like. Who will you be once you no longer feel irritated by your surroundings or unhappy with yourself for being unable to cope? What will you do with your time once you don't have to work frantically just to keep up with daily chores, and when you no longer feel swamped and overwhelmed by all the stuff around you? For some of us, the answers to these questions aren't clear unless we spend a little time thinking about them. And for some of us, the unknown can be a bit unnerving.

Even if you feel quite positive about your un-stuffed future, just believing that things will be better might not be enough to keep you focused and motivated. That's why it can be helpful to figure out some specific results that you can anticipate happily. Maybe you'll have extra time to take a class you've always wanted to take, maybe you'll be able to entertain your friends and family more comfortably, or maybe you just look forward to enjoying a cup of tea every day while sitting quietly in your relaxing surroundings. If you can conjure up a few pleasant images that will be the direct results of your efforts, it will help you get unstuck.

70

Be imperfect:

One thing that definitely will slow down any attack on clutter is the desire for perfection. If we are really fed up with all the stuff surrounding and overwhelming us, it's tempting to charge into un-stuffing with the idea that we're going to make everything absolutely perfect. But the process of disposing of all that stuff we've accumulated usually unfolds in stages. Unless you are the rare soul who can walk away from all that you possess without another thought, you'll hit the wall occasionally as you sort through your things. A wave of sentiment will prevent you from parting with some things, an attack of Good Intentions will slow you down, your spouse will refuse to part with the collection of garden gnomes that has taken over the house as well as the garden.

It's also tempting to be in a rush to correct all the problem areas that we now can see clearly. Some of us can be very goal-oriented and the longer it takes to achieve our new goal of a perfectly organized home, the greater our frustration grows. But the unloading of stuff is a slow and on-going process. It will continue even after we've taken care of every single item we can identify right now because life will continue to send more stuff our way. Some of it will be unwanted, some of it will come by choice or circumstance. As soon as all the mail is sorted and the newspapers tossed out, more is delivered. As soon as the kids' toys are minimized, loving relatives and friends give more. As soon as the basement is cleaned up, we eagerly fill it with all the things we need to pursue our exciting new hobby.

It's important to get comfortable with the process. And it's equally important to be patient with ourselves (and our family or housemates) as we work on it. All we need to do is the best that we can do. Letting go of the idea of attaining perfection is just as important as letting go of stuff. Striving for a comfortable home with a joyous spirit is a far better and more achievable goal.

* * * * *

TIDBIT: IT'S REPLACEABLE

Except for very personal and sentimental items, just about everything that you decide to part with can be replaced easily. So, just because you bought it doesn't mean you need to keep it. You bought it once, you can buy it again if you need it – although you probably won't want to after you've de-junked, un-cluttered and un-stuffed!

* * * * *

MY STORY: TAX PAPER TRAUMA

"You look awful," Lark said as she handed me a tangerine-colored smock.

"Gee, thanks a lot," I replied, only a tiny bit miffed. I knew she was right. But I was grateful finally to be somewhere where I could get some relief from my aches and pains. I clutched the smock and slowly sat down on the massage table in Lark's dimly lit therapy room. My shoulders slumped and my eyelids drooped. I was feeling a bit off, to say the least. "I was up kind of late," I sighed.

"Oh. Was there a problem?" she asked, concerned.

I shrugged and shook my head as if it were nothing important. The truth was that I just didn't know how to explain. Really, all that had happened was that my very good intentions had gone a bit awry. But, at Lark's insistence, I tried my best to relate the events of the previous night.

It seemed that ever since my conversation with Darlene, in which we pledged to get a grip on our overwhelmingly disorganized lives, all I could think about was getting rid of stuff. We had promised to get to work immediately and Darlene had made good on her end of things as soon as she had arrived home. She had barely jetted back into town when she raced to her house, dropped her overnight bag, charged into her kitchen, and immediately tossed out every empty plastic container in the entire place. She estimated that there were about one hundred containers of various sizes, most without lids, and many so flimsy that their usefulness was rather limited anyway. I thought it was a positively grand gesture.

Naturally, I had wanted to make a grand gesture of my own, though I hardly knew where to begin. The opportunities for grand gestures in un-stuffing loomed before me almost anywhere I turned. Finally, I decided to take on a task that I had been avoiding successfully for years. I would get rid of old tax receipts and papers. In this case, I refer to really, really old ones.

As I understand it, the potential for unpleasant correspondence from the Internal Revenue Service concerning one's taxes extends only to those returns filed during the previous seven years. If one has been committing fraud, of course, the IRS reserves the right to be unpleasant for an indefinite period of time. Since I had consistently been fairly scrupulous when it comes to avoiding federal crimes, I felt safe in keeping only seven years worth of evidence regarding our household saving and spending habits.

However, I had always found disposing of all of the old papers and receipts to be a bit of a nuisance. The boxes into which I tossed every possible piece of paper that I thought could be required in an audit inevitably ended up in the furthest reaches of a back closet or the most remote corners of the garage. So I had not exactly kept up to date in my elimination of the unnecessary old material. In fact, once I had tracked down all those scattered boxes, I found that I hadn't disposed of anything for fifteen years. I was compelled to admit that keeping more than twice as much evidence as was required even by the government seemed a bit extreme. I would get to work right away.

Because modern life is so . . . modern, one cannot simply toss one's personal papers into a trashcan. Fear of nosy neighbors pales next to fear of identity theft. That meant that every piece of paper that contained what might be considered private financial information needed be destroyed totally. Of course, one could simply tear each page into teensy little scraps, but I was certain that ripping up eight years worth of papers by hand qualified as a masochistic act.

Years ago, while living in a house with a fireplace, I had tried burning some old papers. It seemed such a simple and direct way to trash them. But I quickly learned that the amount of ashes that papers create is unbelievable. I was forever shoveling the ashes out of the fireplace and onto a compost pile, which soon began to resemble Mount Vesuvius. I also suffered a few small, yet notable singes to my fingers in the process. Most unfortunate, however, was that I chose to burn the papers in July. Almost anywhere in the lower forty-eight states, one really doesn't need a nice, toasty warm fire in July. In the Los Angeles area, I had found it was most certainly superfluous. So, the answer to the question of paper disposal was clearly a paper shredder.

My mother had generously purchased a paper shredder for us as a gift a few years ago. She was undoubtedly hinting that the Writer and I probably could find occasion to use one. Or, perhaps more accurately, she was making it clear that we definitely should find such an occasion. We quickly discovered that we did enjoy having it. There's something very satisfying about shredding a piece of paper into itsy bits. In fact, we enjoyed it so much in day-to-day use that it already had thoroughly crunched its little teeth until they were quite flattened. It had the capacity to shred several sheets at a time when it was new. After its years of frequent use, a few sort of half-hearted little dents were all that appeared in a single sheet of paper as it slid comfortably through the tired old machinery.

So, I cheerfully headed off to the local office supply store to purchase a new shredder. I was met with a surprisingly sophisticated array from which to choose. In the past few years, shredding technology must have advanced nicely. After carefully evaluating the pertinent features, I selected one that would not only speedily gobble up a dozen sheets at a time, but also would remain unfazed if a staple or two slipped through by mistake. It was a weighty, sleek, self-contained model called the Destroyer 3000. It was exactly what I needed.

I set up the new Destroyer in the middle of the living room, which was where I had moved all the old tax boxes. I also had decided that I would take this opportunity to repack the material from the previous seven years, which needed to be saved, into plastic containers for storage. A couple of minor plumbing disasters and one unusually wet winter had impressed upon me in no uncertain terms the value of plastic storage containers for important items.

But just looking at the stacks of fifteen bulky, jam-packed cardboard boxes and seven large, empty plastic ones made my heart begin to race. I immediately noticed that my mouth had become very dry. My forehead was suddenly cold and clammy. Maybe this gesture was too grand. Maybe I should start by cleaning out the glove compartment of my car. Or perhaps my freezer. Or . . .

No. I had the Destroyer. I would not be intimidated. Instead, I decided to name the new shredder "Arnold" and give it a personality appropriate for the namesake of the famous burly actor's popular movie character. I was convinced that it would make the task much more entertaining if Arnold and I were attacking the evil tax receipts together. I pulled out Evil Box Number One and grabbed a handful of Deadly Papers. I shoved them into the jaws of Arnold the Destroyer, and watched with glee as he made short work of them. Our job was clear. We would demolish everything in all of the Evil Boxes. Nothing would stand in our way.

But, as in any good action/adventure movie, there is always something that stands in the way of the hero. For me, even with Arnold's able assistance, there proved to be more than one obstacle. First of all, it appeared that I had stapled every single piece of paper to at least one other piece of paper prior to tossing the lot of them into the boxes. I knew that Arnold could handle a staple or two should that be necessary, but chomping through hundreds, or more likely thousands of them would probably put a quick end to his formidable abilities. So I decided to tear off the corners of all the papers to get rid of the staples. Halfway through tearing corners from the contents of Evil Box Number One, my fingertips already had become disturbingly numb.

More importantly, I discovered that I was easily distracted by the Deadly Papers themselves. As I looked at them, I found I was reliving the moment each one represented. Sometimes it was a moment I'd rather forget. A stack of doctor's bills, for example, does not evoke warm feelings in one's heart. On the other hand, ticket stubs from a trip to the theater brought back memories of a wonderful experience. Since I was regrettably not a person who kept a journal or diary, I decided that I should at least hang on to these happy little mementos of the past. This plan might have worked out well had I not then decided to glance through the appointment calendar for that long past year.

As I perused the pages, I realized that I had quite a decent representation of our history for the entire year, right there in front of me. How lovely it would be to preserve that history in a meaningful way. Suddenly, it occurred to me that this would be the perfect opportunity to start some kind of scrapbook. I could take items like the ticket stubs from each box and then paste them onto pages with all the information gleaned from the appointment calendars, perhaps along with a few lines of personal reminiscences about these special events.

In fact, I concluded, it actually would be extremely efficient for me to dispose of all the unnecessary papers while saving and organizing the mementos at the same time. It would also add an element of fun to an otherwise incredibly tedious and finger-numbing afternoon of shredding with Arnold. I was pleased with my decision. It was clear that this was turning into the kind of grand gesture that would be truly impressive! Now all I needed were some scrapbooking supplies.

Fortunately, I had read in the newspaper that a brand new "Friendly Village Neighborhood Craft Shop" had just opened near the local shopping mall. I would certainly find what I needed there. I gave Arnold a reassuring pat and said, "I'll be back." Then I dashed out the door.

Calling the store a neighborhood craft shop, I discovered, was a slight misnomer. It turned out that the Friendly Village shop was, in reality, about the size of an actual friendly village. There were acres of supplies in an absolutely gigantic warehouse. Artificial flowers and wooden plaques, sequins and beads, clay pots and doll parts, and every other crafty item one could imagine were crammed onto shelves that stretched from floor to ceiling.

I picked up a small shopping basket, then wandered up and down the aisles, mouth agape. Since I am an artist (a dangerous affliction that I plan to discuss further at some later date), I marveled at the creative possibilities before me. "I might as well buy a few tubes of paint while I'm here," I thought, "and maybe a couple of brushes, too."

Later, as I examined a fascinating kit that promised that one could make flawless chocolate candies right in the comfort of one's own home, it occurred to me to check the time. I was appalled to see that I'd been in the Village for an hour and still had not selected my scrapbooking supplies. My shopping basket had mysteriously filled up already, so I hurriedly traded it in on a more appropriately-sized wheeled cart and headed over to what appeared to be the correct aisle.

I must have looked a bit baffled because an unusually helpful employee approached me to see if I had questions. I explained what I wanted to do with my little ticket stubs. The young lady nodded sympathetically, then patiently explained to me that people didn't make scrapbooks anymore, they made "Memory Books." She then kindly provided me with a tour of the many aisles devoted to Memory Book supplies, enthusiastically explaining the options that each of the supplies offered. There were several that were her personal favorites, including the scissors that could cut wavy edges and the small sticky dots that would elevate my little ticket stubs slightly above the page, giving them greater "presence."

I could see that there was a certain sophisticated style that a fine Memory Book clearly required. Wanting my book to be suitably high-caliber, I quickly became caught up in the helpful employee's excitement and the spirit of the adventure. It took only another hour for us to choose my decorative papers, a nice assortment of rubber stamps, a few stencils, and the various other items I would need to create my own fabulously memorable Memory Book.

I wheeled my now fully loaded basket to the checkout stand where I watched, with some chagrin, as the cost of everything was tallied. I swallowed hard, then pulled out a credit card. Well, what price memories? The finished product would surely be worth the substantial amount paid for my visit to the Village.

When I returned home, I unpacked my numerous supplies, spreading them all out on the living room floor so that I could easily select just what I needed at the moment I needed it. How else is an artist supposed to create, for Heaven's sake? Then I decided that everything would move more quickly if I simply dumped all the tax papers on the floor and pulled out all the important Memory Book items first. I was eager to get started on my Memory Book (the fun part) and all this other paper was headed for the recycling center via the jaws of Arnold anyway.

So I opened all the boxes and poured out their contents. Not being foolish, of course, I carefully segregated the important papers and receipts of the previous seven years, which were going into their new plastic containers.

Finally, I sat cross-legged on the floor, surrounded by vast quantities of arts and crafts supplies; one amazingly gigantic pile of papers from the eight superfluous tax years; seven relatively smaller, yet still huge, stacks of papers from the years to be saved; and, of course, Arnold. Also nearby stood the towers of fifteen now empty cardboard boxes and the stack of seven plastic containers. And, in singular glory, on the carpet right before me, was my little pair of theater ticket stubs. I looked around and immediately began to hyperventilate.

At that moment, when the front door opened, only a mild breeze slightly disturbed my carefully placed items. In all honesty, it was not enough to prompt the scream that issued from my lips, followed by my hastily shouted, "Be careful! Be careful!"

The Writer stood quietly for a moment, silhouetted in the doorway. He gently closed the door behind him. Then he slowly commented, "I know there's a reason for this . . ."

I struggled to regain my composure and hastily explained what I was doing.

". . . and so you've caught me right in the midst of my grand gesture," I concluded my story at last and attempted to smile reassuringly.

"Ah," he replied, all too knowingly, I thought. "The grand gesture. I suppose that means I should go pick up Chinese for dinner."

"Well," I agreed demurely, "that would be helpful. But could you use the side door? Please?"

He shook his head, but said nothing. Gingerly making his way through the maze of supplies and boxes and stacks, he maneuvered through the room and out the side door, heading to the garage.

I breathed a sigh of relief that this small crisis had been averted. Now, back to business. I looked at Arnold for reassurance. "It's just you and me, baby," I said, trying my best to sound tough. Then I took the requisite deep breath and began sorting through the enormous pile first, searching for more little ticket stubs and other significant memorabilia.

A couple of hours later, my blood sugar level had hit record lows. I had not wanted to stop for dinner, so I had been working steadily. But I was pleased to realize that much had been accomplished. Arnold had gobbled up pounds of paper. My fingers were only slightly numb. I had successfully accumulated a small pile of appropriately memorable ticket stubs, event flyers, and the like. And, I had started cutting and gluing and stamping the first page of my Memory Book.

The little ticket stubs were indeed elevated above the page by a tiny sticky dot, but it gave them perhaps a less remarkable presence than I had hoped. And yet, the page did look lovely. Already I knew that it was going to be the best Memory Book ever. Even though there was a lot left to do, I felt confident that this was a grand gesture that was working out extremely well.

I decided that it was time to reward myself with a break. I climbed over the stacks and piles, which had multiplied significantly in number as I progressed, thanks to my new system of sorting and stacking by size. This brilliant new system would make tearing out the staples much easier, I thought, when I finally got back to that mundane activity.

Also, although Arnold had done his work well, I found that he generated incredible quantities of little shreds. Already I had completely filled a couple of the empty cardboard boxes with what would have made ample confetti for a fairly long parade. Considering my surroundings, I sensibly made my way rather carefully to the kitchen, where I retrieved the dinner that the Writer had kindly refrigerated for me.

It was a warm night, so dining alfresco seemed a fine idea. I delicately maneuvered back through the living room, very cautiously opened the front door and slipped out onto the porch. The night was still. Not even the tiniest breeze threatened the calm.

I sat on the stoop, contentedly munching Moo Shu Veggies, when Elise strolled by with her golden retriever, Max, in tow. Elise lived next door and had been a good neighbor, so we chatted amiably. Max was always well behaved and, true to form, made only the slightest attempt to share my dinner.

Unfortunately, Brady, Elise's cat, had never been as well behaved as Max. So it should have come as no surprise when Brady leaped out of the bushes and onto my lap, where my Moo Shu comfortably rested. It shouldn't have been a surprise, but it was.

I yelled and jumped up, dumping the Moo Shu onto the porch and flinging Brady off into the air. Brady yeowled as he landed near Max, who was understandably startled. Max lunged and pulled his leash, which was securely wrapped around Elise's hand. In a split second, Elise was flat on the ground and Max was in hot pursuit of Brady. Brady cleverly doubled back past us and squeezed through the tiny opening provided by my slightly ajar front door. Max was a large dog so it took little effort for him to push the door open far enough to follow Brady into the living room. Ah, had I only closed that door . . .

Max and Brady made several loud and frantic circuits at breakneck speed around the living room, wreaking utter havoc on my stacks and piles and craft supplies. Elise and I followed, hopelessly shouting at the animals and sliding around precariously on the slippery papers that spread over the floor and swirled through the air around us as if we were in Times Square on New Year's Eve. All the dog barking and cat screeching and general commotion brought the Writer scurrying down the stairs to investigate. He leaped into the fray as well, finally tackling Max, who by now thought this was just tremendous fun. Max playfully wrestled with the Writer and licked his face. The Writer did not seem to enjoy it.

By the time we had regained control of the situation, Brady, of course, had managed to zip upstairs and hide safely under the bed. We, however, were left in shocked silence amidst the devastation on the living room floor. It was covered by mounds and masses of papers, punctuated here and there by scattered rubber stamps. The confetti had flown onto every surface. The towers of boxes had been felled. Even Arnold had been toppled, and lay forlorn amidst the rubble. A lone stencil rested on him. In gothic script, it read, "Serenity."

Hours later, with the help and kind encouragement of both Elise and the Writer, the tons of papers had been re-stacked, though the stacks most probably were quite random in their contents. Each stack had been stuffed back into a box that had been labeled with the year, which one could only hope had at least some vague affinity to the papers within. The craft supplies had been salvaged and placed in one of the plastic containers, temporarily, of course. The vacuum had done a fair job of cleaning up the confetti. Arnold once again stood proud, ready to devour the contents of the Evil Boxes, which had so rudely triumphed in our recent battle. And I had finally managed to stop sobbing.

"Unbelievable!" Lark exclaimed. She had listened quietly to my entire painful story. "I can see why you need a massage. But now what are you going to do about all those papers?"

I readily admitted that I needed serious help to figure out how to handle this mess. Help that was much tougher than Arnold. Help that was determined and relentless. A force so powerful that disaster wouldn't dare strike again.

Tonight, I would call my mother.

* * * * *

PAPER WEIGHT

By now we all know that the concept of a "paperless society," which was widely heralded with the arrival of the computer age, was only a lovely fantasy. We have more paper in our lives now than we ever did. And we have just as much trouble handling it as we ever did.

If you're like I am, paper is the worst offender in your home when it comes to clutter. I hate dealing with it, so I find all kinds of ways to avoid it. It ends up in piles and stacks and I am always frustrated and annoyed by the mess. Things easily get lost or forgotten, which causes even more frustration. There is an additional danger inherent in stacking piles of papers. First, you need to go through them repeatedly just to remember what's in them, then you re-stack most of them (to deal with them "later"), and when you're done, you believe that you've actually accomplished something because you've spent so much time and energy handling them. But you haven't done anything; it's a total illusion. You still haven't dealt with the papers.

You'd think that it would be easy to toss many of the papers that invade our homes and offices, but for some reason we feel compelled to hang on to every last written word. We keep newspapers, magazines, catalogues, bills, receipts, financial statements, insurance policies, deeds, announcements, invitations, recipes, correspondence, greeting cards, business cards, scraps with phone numbers and other useful information scribbled on them, duplicate copies of duplicate copies, sometimes even flyers stuck on the car's windshield. The truth is that we don't need all of it and the stuff we do keep we don't need to keep as long as we do. Ben Franklin said that time is money, and many of us definitely are wasting huge amounts of both by doing nothing but shuffling and re-shuffling our stacks and piles of papers.

Because paper overload is such a pervasive problem, I would like to offer a few ideas on the subject that I believe can help those of us who suffer from this affliction. Many of these suggestions I learned from my organized mother. In fact, she made an especially noteworthy effort after that unfortunate and rather embarrassing occasion when I had to ask for help shredding my jumbled tax papers. We both now fervently wish that I would put these ideas into practice regularly.

Newspapers, Magazines and Catalogues

There are many items that cause problems for people who have homes overrun by papers, but newspapers, magazines and catalogues are probably the most common offenders. All of them routinely are kept far longer than is necessary.

How long is too long to keep a newspaper? Unless you're saving a week's worth in order to take them to the recycling center, or you're planning to use them within the next few days to pack your things for moving, or you're keeping a couple of sheets to start the fire in your fireplace, there's no reason to keep a newspaper lying around for more than one day. If you didn't read it on the day it arrived, it's not news anymore. If you want to keep an article for future reference or to pass along to a friend (we already know what a dangerous, slippery slope that is), cut it out and file it or hand it off fast. Don't save the whole paper to do it "later." And don't cut out the article and then let it sit on your table for weeks.

How long is too long to keep a magazine? If you're hanging onto one after the next issue comes out, you're going to have to do a few mental gymnastics to justify your decision. Although many of us often don't seem to get much physical exercise, we can become amazingly active when it comes to these mental workouts. Sometimes we keep a magazine because we haven't finished reading every article in it. Is that necessary? Well, we feel we should read all of it because we have a subscription. Is <u>that</u> necessary? Sometimes we automatically renew subscriptions without even thinking about whether or not we want to continue to read the magazine.

On the other hand, if we're keeping a magazine around because we want to finish reading it but we simply have not had the time, this is the time to figure out if that's ever going to happen. Do we need to unload some other time-consuming activities or do we just need to unload the magazine? It truly is okay to toss it into the recycling bin and just let it go.

I keep my favorite magazines in a small wicker basket by the side of the bed. When the stack gets higher than the side of the basket, I know I have to get rid of something. Currently I am holding onto several issues of a magazine I am particularly enjoying. I still go back to each issue to review a few meaningful articles, and I keep thinking I ought to cut out one or two of those articles and file them. If I think about it a little longer, I'm pretty certain that I'll decide that it's wiser to toss the magazines intact and forget about them. That's the particular mental exercise I'm doing right now at the very busy gym in my brain.

Catalogues fall into their own special category. Looking through a catalogue is almost like taking a vacation. It's an opportunity to fantasize about the way we'd love to have our homes look or the beautiful wardrobes we'd enjoy wearing or even just the incredible desserts that we wish we could eat. The power of the images in a well-designed catalogue is just short of hypnotic. And all that is necessary to possess these things that we covet is a toll-free phone call and a credit card number.

Of course, we're not just buying clothing or home decor, for example; we're buying the appealing lifestyle depicted by the models and, through some peculiar twist of our brain cells, we're buying the notion that we (and our lives) will now become just as appealing as they are. It's easy to forget that what we're actually buying is more stuff.

What this means is that a catalogue is a sort of double whammy: not only is it paper that you need to shuffle and probably have a hard time letting go, it's also a potential source of lots more stuff. What a deadly combination! Obviously, the faster you can get it out of your hands, the better off you'll be. So, if you feel that you must peruse a catalogue, enjoy your "vacation," then toss the thing in the trash. You'll get another one in the mail soon enough.

Dealing with the Mail

It's imperative to sort the mail daily when it arrives or as soon as you get home, or you can set aside another specific time to sort it, if you don't come up with an excuse to ignore it again when that time comes. It's helpful to do this in the presence of a large wastebasket and a shredder. Trash the obvious junk immediately – offers for swimming pool accessories, if you don't have a pool; solicitations from worthy causes that you don't intend to support, in spite of the guilt this engenders; real estate agent offers to sell your home, but you're a renter; etc., etc.

Then put the bills that need to be paid in an official bill-paying spot where they won't be forgotten, perhaps a nice little basket or some attractive folder that lessens the offensiveness of its contents. You might even name it – maybe something sophisticated like the "Debit Dossier."

Other mail that requires some kind of action on your part, like an RSVP to a party or a phone call to order tickets to an event, should be put in another official place where you will deal with it when its time comes, too. That can be another attractive little basket or folder as long as it doesn't look exactly like the Debit Dossier. Again, maybe a name would help, such as the "Action Area."

The trickiest part of the Action Area is setting aside the time in which you will take the necessary action. That is the follow-through that is absolutely mandatory in order to have this system work. Otherwise, you end up with nothing but a pile of stuff that overflows your lovely basket and causes more irritation in your life. I haven't conquered this issue yet, though I live in constant hope.

Finally, resist with all your heart and might the temptation to save interesting mail that you want to "think about." If the local theater group sends its entire yearlong schedule in an elaborately printed brochure and you honestly believe that you might like to go once in awhile, put the fancy brochure in the Action Area and act on it quickly. Don't keep it around for six months while you continue to ponder the possibilities whenever you run across it. The theater group undoubtedly advertises its performances regularly in your city's newspaper and you also probably can find all that you need to know about the schedule online. Get rid of the brochure. Please! It will only torture you if you don't.

If your favorite charity kindly sends you free return address labels with your name, address and some drawings of cuddly pandas on them, you are not required either to keep or use those labels. Yes, I can confirm that they may be tossed out without severe moral or legal consequences. If you decide that you will use them, put them in yet another cute little container which stores your stamps, your vast collection of charmingly illustrated return address labels from other charities, and perhaps a few paper clips and rubber bands. If you're still enamored of alliteration, you may wish to refer to this as your "Mail Manager."

Paying Your Bills

After you finally force yourself to sit down and pay the bills you have amassed in your Debit Dossier, you will be left with many things that need to be filed. Maybe. Shocking as this may sound, you may choose not to file a stub from every single bill that you pay. Your cancelled check is all the proof that you need to show if there is a dispute with the company, which is relatively rare anyway. So why keep all that extra paper? And if you're doing business with a bank that keeps all your checks that you've written, you've eliminated even more paperwork. You can always request a copy of a check if it's ever an issue, so all you really may need to have in your possession is a well-maintained checkbook ledger.

If you require something to bolster your tax deduction claims, the extra paper backup could be worthwhile. However, if you fear that the gas company will discontinue your service unless you can document the last five years that you've been a customer, with billing stubs, in their original mailing envelopes, you may want to enlist the assistance of someone who can help you get a better grip on reality.

An additional brilliant idea I proudly claim as my own is to put the household's account number on a card that has the company's name and phone number on it and keep all the information in my

Rolodex. Having the account number right there in front of me is quite handy if I need to call the company with a question or request. I also never need to call to find out a billing address, if I've somehow managed to remember to include that on the card. An organized person may think this is such an obvious thing to do that it doesn't even bear mentioning, but I offer it unashamed to others who struggle with annoying paperwork as much as I do.

Probably the best idea I ever implemented regarding paying bills was signing up for an automatic online bill paying service linked to my checking account. For a reasonable fee, most of the basic household bills are sent directly to this service. I don't even have to look at them in paper form, though I still can see them in detail online and, of course, I can download them for printing if I want to defeat the whole purpose of the service.

I can instruct the service to pay a bill automatically if the amount falls within a range I specify. For example, my cellular phone bill comes in at about the same amount every month, so I've instructed the bill paying service to pay it automatically if the bill is at or under that amount. For other bills with varying amounts, like credit cards, I may initiate payment manually. Every time a bill is received by the service, I get e-mail telling me that it's arrived; every time a bill is paid by the service, I get e-mail telling me that it's been paid, along with a confirmation number. It's fabulous! I'm never late with a payment and I deal with far less paper.

There are also online banking services available that allow you to pay your bills via your computer, although the bills continue to be mailed to you. In addition, many companies offer their own direct, paperless online billing and payment services, or pay-by-phone services. Any of these options simplify bill paying and cut paperwork, so they're worth considering if you're a paperwork procrastinator.

Filing What Needs to be Kept

Filing is truly one of the most boring activities I can imagine. I have tried several kinds of filing systems, but none of them worked for me. There was one that used color-coded file folders, but that required a large stockpile of different colored folders. Maybe I used too many colors, but they took up far too much space.

Another version of the color-coding system used colored labels, which at least meant that the stockpile was smaller. But I would run out of one or two colors before I'd used up all the others. Then I'd forget to buy more at the store and so I'd improvise, which was just inviting trouble. It also offended my desire for perfection, ludicrous as that sounds. I truly wanted those files to be neat and orderly, and I'd get distressed that I was messing up my system. I've also learned that labels don't stay sticky forever. Eventually they become useless, or worse, fall off of older files, leaving a mystery file in the midst of all the others.

There was also one very detailed system that I tried briefly that used a Master File List. This seemed like a lot of extra work to add to something that was already an extremely annoying task. It quickly proved beyond the limits of my patience.

So I came up with my own simplified plan which I now humbly share with you. The first issue to address is figuring out how much stuff you need to file. It's less than you already have packed into your cabinets. Start by throwing away every single piece of paper that you can't justify keeping. And don't settle for the wimpy excuses you'll initially come up with for hanging onto something that should go. Just because you actually took the trouble to file those now expired insurance policies, those outdated catalogues, and those travel brochures for places you no longer even care to visit, doesn't mean that you should keep them. This de-junking effort alone should clear up a good-sized chunk of filing space.

When, in the future, you are considering saving something to file, first ask yourself if it's absolutely necessary to keep the item. Remember that most paperwork is replaceable and quite often the information in it can be obtained from other sources. With a bit of thought, you might decide that the item is trashable. If you're undecided, you also might consider scanning it and saving it in paperless form on your computer.

If you have specific business needs, obviously you'll require space for those business files, which could include anything from client records to invoices to sales brochures. However, once again remember that whatever you can keep track of with a computer program will minimize your paper shuffling and necessary filing space.

If you have tax deductible business expenses, it will work to your advantage to keep the necessary receipts filed by category so you don't have to spend hours and hours figuring out this information at tax time. Computer programs that track your expenses by category are great for this purpose. If you use the program meticulously and then you want to be cavalier about your receipts, it's okay. You can toss them all in a box and forget about them unless you get audited. Of course, for mysterious reasons far beyond my comprehension, I can pretty much guarantee that you will, in fact, get audited if you do this. Then you'll be stuck sorting the cursed receipts anyway. At the very least, your accountant will be horrified to learn of your sloppy record keeping. But desperate measures might be called for in some cases and I would be the last one to criticize should anyone choose to handle their affairs this way.

Clearly, it's very important to get really friendly with your computer. Find someone who can help you if you're uncomfortable with technology. I thank Heaven that I have the Writer available to explain things to me when I am in a state of total confusion. I am particularly grateful because my computer actually is an alien life form in disguise that frequently will not obey my commands and secretly laughs at my ignorance. (The Writer vehemently denies this, but I am still suspicious.)

If you don't have the good fortune to have a computer literate partner or spouse, and you do have a young family, your twelve-year-old will be able to help you. If you have resistance to the idea of turning to your child for help, just remember that you are still the one who can drive the car.

Let's move on to your personal files, which you should keep separate from your business files, either in a different drawer or different cabinet if you have quite a lot of files. If this is the case, maybe you should go back one more time and try to figure out why you have so many files in the first place.

Most people will need to include space for things like life insurance policies, health insurance claims and payments, some banking and investing information, and whatever else is deemed truly important. For example, I have a file devoted to warranties for household appliances and a bunch of files that contain instruction manuals for computer peripherals and programs. Sometimes I even manage to keep these files up to date, which I consider a very fine accomplishment. I also have a small file that contains a couple dozen magazine and newspaper cartoons that I find hysterically funny. It's a great one to pull out on a not-so-great day. If I were extremely efficient, I might scan each of the cartoons so I could just call them up on my computer whenever I felt like it. But, I confess that I enjoy having them in their printed form, so I'm willing to let them take up a bit of cabinet space.

Now, my system to eliminate filing hassles:

Come up with big categories that work for you like "Insurance" and "Banking" and "Health," and put those category titles in the little plastic tab labels for hanging files; put the hanging files in alphabetical order in your cabinet.

Make manila file folders for smaller, more specific categories and label them with, for example, the name of your bank or your life insurance company; then file all the manila folders within the hanging files. If you have several manila folders that fit into one hanging file, place them in there in alphabetical order.

Finally, place your individual documents to be filed in the appropriate manila folders and, voila! You are done.

In spite of this impressive knowledge of advanced filing technique, I currently face several piles of papers requiring my attention. With such a clean and simple system as the one I've described, you might wonder why it doesn't work perfectly for me all of the time. Step Three is the obstacle; one must actually <u>file</u>. However, if that hurdle can be overcome through the sheer force of will and self-discipline, I can assure you that this system will prove to be quite adequate.

Personal Papers: Correspondence and Greeting Cards

There's nothing quite like a hand-written letter. In our time, unfortunately, it seems to be such a rare species of writing that it's just about extinct. If you have some old hand-written letters, they're probably worth saving just for historical reference. But since we now know that we must keep only what we use or love, even letters need to be scrutinized with those qualities in mind. Often there may be a sentimental issue involved that makes you feel that you want to hold onto all of your letters, but remember that saving the letter isn't required in order to keep the sentiment alive. After a bit of soul-searching you may eventually decide that it's perfectly fine to toss even the hand-written stuff. If not, at least tie the letters all together with a lovely bow and keep them in a special place where you can read them whenever you feel the need.

The same is true of greeting cards. A card is sent to cheer you, or to celebrate a milestone or holiday. While the cards may be beautiful or funny or moving, we must acknowledge that particular time has past. You may treasure the memories of the occasion, but it's perfectly okay to let the cards go.

Special Paper Category #1: Photographs

Photos need to be handled just like any other paper that you encounter. Bad ones can be tossed away; good ones should be filed, only in the case of photographs, we usually think in terms of filing them in an album or one of those decorative photo storage boxes. We think in those terms, but often we fail to follow through.

Of course, dealing with photographs can break down long before we get to the album stage. If we have used a traditional camera, the film must be developed and printed. It cannot provide much joy sitting in its little canister. (And isn't it hard to toss away those little canisters? There must be something that we could do with them . . .)

But even if we do manage to get them printed, handling photographs seems to make otherwise sensible people lose their decision-making capabilities. Let's say we have a photo of Aunt Tilly in which the top half of her head is all that's visible. The head is situated in the lower left corner of the frame and the rest of the picture provides a superb view of the sky on the day that the picture was taken. Now, you'd think it would be easy to toss that photo out. But no, it's dear old Aunt Tilly, we tell ourselves, so we must keep the picture. So, usually we put it in the back of the stack and put the stack back in its envelope to deal with "later." Or, if we're very organized and putting the photos in an album, we hide this bad photo in the same slot behind one of the good ones, "just in case."

I am unclear under what circumstances we might want to pull that bad photo out, if we ever even remember that it's hiding in there. Perhaps someday we'll cut it up and make a collage of Aunt Tilly using all the many pictures we have of her in which other parts of her anatomy are the only things visible. Barring that ambitious project, perhaps we should just let go of the pathetic picture.

If we are using a digital camera, the process is allegedly simpler because the pictures can be transferred immediately to our computer. If we resist the temptation to tinker with them in one of the many programs designed to improve upon our limited photographic skills, they can be viewed and sent immediately via e-mail to everyone we care to include on our mailing list.

However, unless we want the family to gather 'round the monitor every time we'd like to share our photos, we still might want to print some of them. So we're back to paper again. I am hopeful that we would be more disciplined about printing and choose only the good ones. And yet I would bet that a digital photo of Aunt Tilly with exactly the same problems described above wouldn't be deleted from its computer file, either, "just in case" we wanted to print it. Ah, well. At least its storage is a far less significant problem.

Special Paper Category #2: Books

I always have a difficult time parting with my books. I love to read and if I had a large enough home, I would devote one entire room to a library. I would keep in my library every single book I have ever read and loved. It would be a massive collection and I would walk back and forth through the "stacks" regularly, remembering how much I enjoyed reading all those wonderful books.

Alas, reality requires winnowing my collection regularly in order to fit it into a few bookcases. Fortunately, public libraries do exist and they are devoted to keeping lots of books on hand for us. There are also plenty of bookstores that will keep the flow of new material readily available.

I think that the easiest way to convince yourself to part with your books is to realize that you're just passing them on to someone else to read and enjoy, too. Make a little extra cash by taking them to your neighborhood used bookstore or make the local library very happy with a donation of books for their next used book fundraising sale.

A Final Thought about Papers

All of the papers that you've decided to keep need a home of their own. As long as you've sorted and tossed the excess stuff first, buying bookcases, filing cabinets, photo albums, decorative boxes, whatever is appropriate for your paper goods, is a worthwhile storage investment. Keep in mind that convenient access to all of your paper stuff makes dealing with it much easier. Once you set up your own way to handle your papers, all that's left is the handling. Unfortunately, I still haven't found a way around that. Of course, someday I hope to win the lottery and hire someone to take care of the whole thing for me.

* * * * *

TIDBIT: OFFICE SUPPLIES

You don't need to keep twenty-five boxes of plastic tabs and their paper inserts to label your hanging files. You don't need fifty pens. You don't need twelve boxes of staples or five thousand paper clips or seventeen reams of printer paper. There is a handy facility called the "office supply store" that will keep all of that stuff for you. Then, when you're down to your last few pens or last hunk of printer paper, you can go to the store and purchase the small amount that you honestly have room for in your office. Let the store be your storeroom!

* * * * *

TRUE CONFESSIONS: COUPONS

If you're long on time and short on money, coupons are a good way to save a few dollars – unless you're in the middle of a Stuff Attack, a condition that I know all too well. Then coupons are just more annoying pieces of paper. That's why I had to give up on using them.

In all honesty, I must say that I never have been able to handle coupons properly. Whenever I was at the store, I almost never remembered that I had them, even if I somehow miraculously had remembered to put them in my purse. When I got to a checkout stand, some powerful hypnotic force must have taken over my brain because all I could do was stare numbly as the items got totaled up. I would pay, walk out to my car, and that's when I would remember the fifty-cents-off coupon for orange juice that I could have used.

I know that there are cute little organizers that you're supposed to stick in your purse that allegedly help keep your coupons straight, but things started to fall apart for me long before I got to that stage.

In the past, the typical scenario was that I would look through the coupons in the newspaper, clip out the relevant ones (along with several irrelevant ones that caught my eye, as if I really needed a cheap five-pound tub of peanut butter), then put them . . . somewhere. Often they'd just get lost in the mounds of paper that engulfed numerous surfaces throughout the house.

Sometimes I'd make an envelope labeled "Coupons" and optimistically stick it in the kitchen "junk drawer" where it would be ready for me when I needed it. Of course, I'd rarely remember to check the envelope. When I did get around to it, the coupons had inevitably expired and I inevitably felt irritated and a bit ridiculous.

Now the only coupons I use are from a home decorating store that inundates my mailbox with offers of five-dollars off my next fifteen dollar purchase. Five dollars is a more significant amount to save than the average twenty-five or fifty-cents at the grocery store, so I usually do manage to take advantage of their generosity when I shop there. Also, their coupons are huge, cardboard-like things that are hard to miss. I keep them in a bag in my car. Sometimes I have to make an extra trip back to the car to get one, but I guess five bucks is enough of a motivator to make me remember that they're there.

So, now when I see other coupons, I ignore them. I got tired of feeling bad about myself because I kept forgetting to use them. To me they were just more stuff, so I decided that abandoning the whole idea was a lot cheaper than paying a therapist.

* * * * *

TRUE CONFESSIONS: DIGITAL DILEMMA

The Writer has his own clutter complaint that is currently frustrating him. He uses his computer to do all kinds of things in addition to writing, including making computer animation. Because that sort of work is brain intensive for the computer as well as for him, he now has a couple of hard drives that are packed with important digital information. He needs to make some decisions about what he's going to keep and how he's going to store it, including how to best organize his storage system.

There's no escaping! Even in digital form, there can be too much stuff. But don't despair. At least it doesn't take up a lot of square footage in your home!

* * * * *

TRUE CONFESSIONS: FASHION

Fashion is an area in which I have zero expertise. Most of the time, I try to look presentable; sometimes I even succeed. But I am just not a woman who adores shopping and has eighty-seven pairs of shoes in her closet. I don't have bags to match every outfit, or even very many outfits, beyond my matching sweats and their summertime counterparts in lighter-weight materials.

Obviously, I live a minimalist fashion existence, though it's not through lack of trying. It's just that I discovered early on that I simply don't have much of a knack for artfully putting together cutting edge, insouciant little ensembles that would dazzle my many admirers. Fortunately, I work at home and I have learned that almost anyone can assemble a few reasonable meeting outfits and "dress-up" clothes, even if one is completely unequipped to cope with the demands of an acceptable daily wardrobe.

My friend Maddy's "think pink, buy black" clothing rule has been a lifesaver for me. If you restrict your wardrobe almost exclusively to black, it simplifies both shopping and getting dressed. Since I have always needed simplification wherever I could get it, I became an ardent follower. I found that sticking with the Rule helped me minimize closet clutter. Minimize but not eliminate. I'm human and I have lapses. Recently when I was shopping for some new spring togs, I was in a cheerful mood and found myself violating the Rule, big time. I bought a set of pink sweats. Well, they aren't exactly pink; they're "melon." Regrettably, when I put them on at home, I realized that I felt like a cantaloupe. Still, I was a rather cheerful cantaloupe, so for now the sweats will remain in my wardrobe – though I won't wear them when I see Maddy.

* * * * *

THE CLUTTERED CLOTHES CLOSET

Whether you faithfully "think pink, buy black" or choose to fill your closet with bold splashes of colors, whether you're a fashion disaster or a fashion tastemaker, whether you're a man or a woman, it's safe to assume that you have too many clothes. You have things in your closet that don't fit, things that are worn out, things that are truly ugly. It's an affliction that burdens the vast majority of Stuff Sufferers as well as plenty of otherwise organized people. But even if you agree wholeheartedly that something's got to go, you'll find that the sorting and tossing process for your clothes closet can be derailed by the same wrong-thinking traps that slow us down in other areas.

So, after you've pulled out the obviously hopeless rags and set aside the really good pieces that you love, if you find that eighty percent of your clothes are still hanging there, it's time to address the reasons why you're still hanging on. I would bet that you'll find your excuses right here among the familiar ones that I have to battle, too:

"It just needs to be fixed – altered/mended/a button put on."

If this is the honest truth, set it aside and alter or mend or put the stupid button on the thing and wear it already! What possible good is it doing trapped in some sort of limbo in your closet? Personally, I have achieved unbelievable heights of procrastination when it comes to these small obstacles. I finally concluded that it's worth a few dollars to take the item to the seamstress at the local dry cleaning shop and have her fix it. Sometimes delegating a task is the best way to handle it. Sometimes it's the only way.

"It will come back in style if I keep it long enough."

No, it probably won't. And it definitely won't come back at a time when <u>you</u> should be wearing it. We've all seen retro-chic items on the very young, who seem to get a perverse temporary thrill out of the previous generation's most extreme fashion statements. But the sad fact is that it doesn't mean the look will work for you if you are old enough to have worn it the first time around. Very stylish items are very much of their era and you'll just look like you forgot to change with the times.

"If I buy a skirt (or pants or shoes, etc.) to match it, it will be perfectly fine."

You must be careful because you can go completely broke following this line of logic. You take an item that doesn't work and buy more items that don't work to make an entire ensemble that . . . doesn't work. Trust me; this plan doesn't work.

"But it was expensive. I can't afford not to wear it!"

You can't afford to wear it if it's all wrong. It doesn't matter how much you paid for something if you look awful or terribly outdated in it. You'll just look like a person with a substantial disposable income who doesn't have a clue how to shop. If it is a very pricey item, you could take it to a resale shop. But don't kid yourself about the resale value of anything that isn't from a designer label. If it's just expensive, give a friend or relative an enormous charge by passing it along. But make sure that it's appropriate for the recipient's style. We're all in this together and it's bad form to contribute to anyone else's fashion problems.

"But it's perfectly good. It's so wasteful to get rid of it."

There must be some reason that you're not wearing it if it's perfectly good. Maybe it doesn't fit properly or it looks unattractive on you. Or maybe it just has some bad memories attached to it — you wore it to your divorce settlement hearing or on the day that you got fired. Sometimes a memory is so powerful that it is impossible to separate it from the garment you were wearing at the time. Whatever your reason, what's wasteful is letting clothing hang there unworn when you could hand it off to a friend or donate it to charity so that someone else could use and enjoy it.

"My boyfriend/mother/best friend gave it to me"—or worse "made it for me."

When treading on sentimental ground, it's crucial to remember that it is not the gift but the thoughtfulness of the giver that is significant. The item itself, no matter what it is, is just a symbol of caring, which is lovely. But the awareness and memory of that caring is what has true value. I am a sucker for sentimental stuff and confess that I still have a few items stashed away for that very reason. If you simply can't part with them, that's the only way to handle these clinging vines – tuck them away where at least they're not taking up valuable closet space.

"I'm planning to make a quilt/curtains/doggy coat out of the material someday."

When was the last time you sewed anything? If there were even a remote possibility that you were going to use the item in question for any of those purposes, wouldn't you have done it by now? I am embarrassed to confess that I only recently parted with a lovely piece of fabric from a fancy gown I wore in . . . high school. It also had sentimental value, so that compounded my attachment and contributed to what I now realize was an utter delusion. Especially since I don't sew.

"I'll just wear it around the house."

There are two reasons why this is an extremely poor excuse to hang onto some usually very disreputable clothes. First of all, you hardly ever wear something around the house, other than your jammies, that you won't wear in public someday if you're in a hurry, or in a bind, or just in a lousy mood. It seems you can always justify a quick trip to the store or to pick up the kids while you're in your "around the house" outfit.

But I can guarantee that on one of those days when you are looking exceptionally raggedy, you will run right into your highly critical boss or your hostile ex-in-laws or the charming new neighbor you'd so hoped to impress. I know I've seen far too many people I didn't want to see when I was wearing something I didn't want to be seen in.

Second, even if you are alone in the house and are not subjecting your Significant Other or other family members or roommates to your appalling lack of style, you have to look at you. As a person who is coping with a house full of too much stuff and too many things, it's easy to feel so overwhelmed that getting dressed at all can seem like a triumph. I understand and sympathize completely. There are times when I feel like spending the entire day in my terrycloth robe and fuzzy bunny slippers, too. But cleaning out the closet gives us an opportunity to make sure that we have clothes that make us look "decent," as my Mom's generation used to say. If we make the effort to wear them, they can help us feel a healthy dose of self-respect. We don't have to dress as if we're in a sitcom from the fifties, but we do deserve and need to honor ourselves.

"As soon as I lose weight, it will fit perfectly."

This must be the most often used excuse for hanging on to clothes that don't work. But in most cases when we keep items that are too small, we're not really holding on to the clothes, we're holding on to the fantasy that those clothes represent. We used to be able to wear a size five or we've always wanted to be able to wear a size five and if we let those clothes go, we're giving up on the idea of ever being able to wear a size five.

The truth is that it's perfectly okay to be the size you are, whatever size that is. Of course, if you have a weight problem that jeopardizes your health, it's certainly a good idea to try to deal with the situation. But right here and right now, at whatever weight you are, you need to have clothes that fit you and make you feel good about yourself. You don't need something that tortures you every time you look at it, which is what the small stuff does to many of us who keep it around. Better to let it go and get on with real life. And in the future, if you ever happen to be a size five, you'll have loads of fun shopping for brand new clothes.

Sometimes we keep an old piece of clothing that's too small because it represents the past. If we give it up, we feel like we're giving up our youth. This is an extremely personal variation of the Sentimental Trap. I don't happen to know anyone who joyously embraces all the aspects of getting older, but a certain amount of graceful acceptance of the passage of time seems like the most elegant way to handle aging. When I was younger, I could squeeze into a much smaller dress size, but my life experience was much smaller, too. And since I can't turn back the clock anyway, I think I'll just try to be content with my hard-won bits of wisdom and my wider hips.

Of all the items we need to sort and toss, clothes are some of the easiest items to dispose of – there are so many charities that are delighted to receive still-wearable clothing. And there's absolutely no doubt that someone will be grateful to have your donated things. We can help them out and at the same time help ourselves to some much-needed breathing room in our overstuffed closets.

* * * * *

TIDBIT: DETAILS

Don't get derailed in your un-cluttering efforts by some small detail. If, for example, you're cleaning out your clothes closet and run across a shoebox full of souvenirs from your last vacation, don't start sorting through the souvenirs. Stay focused on the job of deciding what clothes you're keeping and what ones you're tossing. You can deal with all the other things that you've stashed in that closet at a later date.

* * * * *

TIDBIT: CARRYING CLUTTER

Do you know what's in your purse?
Any idea of what's in your briefcase?
Do you have a clue what's in the trunk of your car?

Are you carrying your over-stuffed, cluttered life everywhere you go? You're un-cluttering your house, so why not unburden yourself, too? Toss all that excess stuff you're hauling around and get on with life!

* * * * *

STUFF ON THE GO

About the only time we're guaranteed to be acutely aware of how much stuff we have is when we're at the airport, dragging a ton of it with us to the ticket counter to check in. At least we're never alone in our plight. Long lines of travelers with huge mounds of bags are a staple of almost any air travel experience.

Of course, in the days before carry-on bag limitations, anyone who ever traveled undoubtedly encountered a fellow passenger who decided he would just skip that checking-in part. Instead, he'd bring his stuff right on the plane with him and pack it in the overhead compartments. The fact that he alone could fill the compartments over several aisles never seemed to hold him back. Usually he would bring on lots of shopping bags filled with all kinds of stuff that would spill out during the boarding process. Frequently there'd be some oversized thing, a stuffed animal, perhaps, or a fragile, odd-shaped decorative piece that he intended to hang over the mantle back home. After taking lots of time and requiring the assistance of most of the flight attendants, he'd spread out all the remaining stuff in his seating area, which too often was right next to ours.

But even though we're now all restricted to a small carry-on bag, many of us are still successfully hauling along a huge amount of stuff when we go on a trip. We check the maximum amount of baggage allowed, knowing that each bag is packed full to the brim. Maybe we're even willing to pay more so we can check an extra bag or two. Some of us don't want to be bothered with check-in, so, if we can afford it, instead we ship our stuff ahead so that it's there waiting for us when we arrive. Whatever the cost, whatever it takes, we're determined to get as much stuff as possible to our destination.

It doesn't matter where we're going, the packing routine is the same. We pack carefully to allow for any possible weather variations. What if it's hot? Lightweight clothing. What if it gets chilly? Extra sweaters and jackets. We prepare for casual days and dressy occasions. Then there are accessories, casual and dressy, of course. Shoes and boots for every situation we might encounter. Nightgowns and pajamas. Make-up and shaving items, and other toiletries, too.

Better take everything, including that facial mask we never have time for at home. Medicines and vitamins, special hats for the beach or the ski slopes or the lake, a few paperbacks to read on the plane and at the hotel, some toys and games for the kids to keep them occupied. In fact, we usually decide that we should shop in advance of our trip to make sure that we have enough stuff so that all the possibilities definitely are covered.

If we're traveling by car, we're just as determined to fill every available square inch of space in the trunk, on the floor, in the back seat, even strapped onto the roof. We squeeze ourselves in between loads of luggage, bags of snacks, ice chests full of sodas, and, on occasion, maybe a little camping gear. Being able to drive the car comfortably is a secondary concern; most important is making sure that it's fully stuffed.

If we own one of those elaborate campers, we can take almost our entire home, or at least a miniaturized version of it, right along with us. There's even room for some decorative stuff in the flashier models. And there's no way that space won't be used.

Most of us probably have learned from experience that we take far too much stuff with us when we're travelling. Dragging it all along the way slows us down and often results in extra expense that we could have avoided. Once we arrive at our destination, half the time we don't even get the stuff fully unpacked. Then hauling it all back home makes us feel a bit silly, so we vow that next time we'll do a better job of packing. Sometimes we do, but it seems we have a tendency to repeat our mistakes quite a few times before we finally figure out that we don't need to bring along an entire household's worth of goods every time we take to the road.

Once, years ago, I was packing for a trip back home to visit my family. As usual, I was determined to bring along everything that I might want, which was always more than I ever actually needed. The Writer watched, amused, as I loaded up my case of make-up and toiletries to the point that it wouldn't zip shut. He finally commented wryly, "You know, they have stores now in Colorado." I was not immediately appreciative of his observation at the time but, of course, he was right. I was packing far more than was necessary.

On another occasion, heading back home once again, I was much wiser. As an experiment, I decided to see just how little I could take and still get by comfortably. I was amazed and pleased to discover that a five-day trip required only the backpack that I carried daily and a small carry-on bag. I felt remarkably unburdened on that particular visit.

It turns out that the less stuff you carry with you, the less you have to think about. Your choices are limited, so you get a bit creative. You mix and match things in ways that you might not think of at home. Your find that your trip is not ruined if you wear the same outfit more than once. If you forget some little item, you pick it up at a local shop. If you're going to multiple destinations, it's a breeze. Easy to re-pack, easy to carry, easy to get on with the whole reason that you're on a vacation: vacationing.

In fact, when we're on vacation, a night at a hotel can offer a glimpse into how we honestly feel about all that stuff we left behind. Even if we hauled a truckload of stuff with us, the majority of what we own is nowhere to be seen. Rarely is any of it missed. In fact, most of us revel in the simplified environment of a hotel room. It may be the only time that we get any relief from that suffocating feeling caused by all the clutter that surrounds us at home.

And yet, whenever we go on vacation it seems that we always want to bring more stuff back with us: souvenirs. Of course, we don't often carefully select one special item to cherish along with our memories. Instead we load up on all kinds of things, many of them inexpensive trinkets and decorative junk which we then have to make room for in our already crowded homes.

We also usually take tons of photographs that we sometimes actually manage to get printed, but we don't often get placed in a photo album. We bring back brochures from the attractions on the sight-seeing trips we took, along with lots of postcards that didn't get mailed, and maybe even a menu or two from a restaurant we really enjoyed. I once knew a couple who loved to dine out so much that when they traveled they photographed their plates of food as they were served in every new restaurant!

Souvenirs can be wonderful mementos of joyous times, but they don't bring much joy if they just add more stuff to our overstuffed homes or if they aren't available for us to access easily. On your next vacation, before you buy them and stash them away in your suitcase, it's worth figuring out exactly what you'll do with your souvenirs when you get back home.

Souvenirs should fit on your inventory list, just like everything else you have in your home. Maybe it really is important to you to hold onto those Broadway show ticket stubs, or buy a handmade woolen sweater in Ireland, or save a few beads from Mardi Gras. As always, whatever you want to keep is something that only you can decide. But it's a good idea to make it a thoughtful choice.

How much stuff do you really need to preserve your happy vacation memories? Probably not very much at all.

* * * * *

TIDBIT: MOVING

A friend of ours who recently had to move across the country on short notice is telling everyone that if there's a move in their future, they should start preparing six months in advance. For those of us laden with tons of stuff and things, six months is probably cutting it pretty close.

Even if you're convinced that you'll never leave your particular homestead, we all must acknowledge that we do live in a very mobile society and life has been known to toss some unexpected curves. It would be much nicer if you were un-stuffed well in advance of any changes of location.

If you look around your home and figure out what it would take to move, my guess is that will be pretty motivating to get you started unloading all your unnecessary things right now.

* * * * *

TRUE CONFESSIONS: TRAPPED

Many years ago my elderly former neighbors faced a dilemma. They were a retired couple who lived in a charming house that was filled with the accumulated stuff of a lifetime – large pieces of furniture, paintings, and lovely decorative items from their many travels. They had been offered a wonderful opportunity to move back to the East Coast and live in a small apartment close to friends and family they dearly loved. But they chose not to make the move. Why? They didn't know what they would do with all of their stuff. How sad. Would you sacrifice some of your favorite things in order to be close to those people you care about, or would you be trapped by your possessions?

* * * * *

"An object in possession seldom retains the same charm that it had in pursuit."

Pliny the Younger
62-114

HOBBLED BY HOBBIES

Almost everyone at one time or another develops an interest in some kind of hobby. It's the one area of life in which we get to choose exactly what we'd like to do and, as a result, it can guarantee us a unique kind of personal satisfaction that we might not get anywhere else. One other thing that's guaranteed, however, is that no matter what the hobby may be, there will be plenty of stuff associated with it.

We usually assume that some hobbies like sports, or sewing, or arts and crafts require lots of stuff, with special equipment and supplies that can take up quite a bit of space and cost a fair amount of money. But let's examine an example of a pastime that most of us probably think would be fairly inexpensive and generate a relatively small amount of stuff around the home. What might happen if you enjoy playing bridge as your hobby? You, too, may not be off the hook when it comes to accumulating stuff.

You've taken lessons at the local community center so you've got the basics down and have met some fellow enthusiasts. A couple of decks of cards, maybe a book or two on the subject and a handful of friends who also play the game ought to do the trick for starters.

But as you get more immersed in your hobby, you're eager to learn and want to improve your playing so you start to acquire more instructional books. Soon you begin to think of your books as a collection and decide to try to get a copy of every book ever written on how to play the game. Of course, since you're technologically adept you also purchase a bridge game or two for your computer, and a little handheld gaming device that lets you play bridge on your own while you're travelling or stuck waiting for someone. You also decide to cut out all the articles in the local newspaper's bridge column and file them away for "future reference."

Then you think it would be fun to add a few jaunty items to your wardrobe, maybe a tee shirt or sweatshirt or two with some catchy card-playing slogan across the front, or a baseball cap with an embroidered deck of cards on it. You begin to host bridge parties at your home, so you decide to purchase a special set of dishes, also decorated with playing cards, just for those occasions, along with drinking glasses, and a matching tablecloth and napkins. While shopping, you discover some cute little trinkets designed especially for card players that would be perfect to decorate your luncheon table. Why not get those, too?

You join a more formal bridge club, where soon you are installed as an officer, with a little corsage or perhaps a pin as a memento of the occasion. Better start a scrapbook and maybe include some photos of your bridge-playing partners. And aren't there some special scrapbooking pages and decorations that you could use?

You decide to subscribe to periodicals about bridge and you save them, again, for future reference. A successful tournament or two bring in a trophy or medal. Could certificates of achievement and master points earned be far behind?

Your friends are aware of your hobby, so they begin to purchase gifts for you that they think are appropriate, like a ceramic figurine of a child pondering a handful of playing cards while her puzzled puppy looks up at her. Your co-worker gets you a plaque for your kitchen that says, "No cooking tonight – Bridge game in progress!" Your kids buy a welcome mat for your front door that has a fanned out deck of cards on it and "Bridge Players Live Here" in large, boldface type.

Eventually you become so enamored of the game that you travel on your vacations, at no small expense, to tournaments around the country. You decorate your luggage with appropriate stickers proclaiming that you're a bridge player and you pick up little souvenirs on your trips to add to your growing collection of bridge playing knick-knacks back home.

One day you turn to your spouse and suggest that you redecorate the den to reflect your bridge playing enthusiasm. Maybe you could get some new furniture, including a special card playing table and chairs, and set up a small bar with a refrigerator so that snacks are available without a trip to the kitchen.

And the list goes on endlessly.

Now, let me make it clear that I think there is absolutely nothing wrong with any of this and, no, I'm not just picking on bridge players – my own Mom teaches bridge! If you love your hobby, whatever it may be, and want to acquire all kinds of stuff that makes it even more pleasurable and shows the world what your interests are, good for you. Enjoy! Enjoy!

My point is that we live in a completely consumer-oriented culture. That means that everywhere you turn, no matter what your interests, there will be plenty of enticement and opportunity for you to add more stuff to your home and your life. What's important is to be aware of this fact and make decisions about what you accumulate based on what you need and what will bring you happiness whenever you use it or look at it. Otherwise, it's very easy for your hobby to take over your house with a bunch of mindlessly gathered stuff that ends up as nothing more than useless clutter. And you thought you were just interested in playing an innocent game of cards!

Another common danger associated with hobbies is that you can lose interest but not lose all the stuff that you gathered around you when you first started to pursue your hobby. Sometimes it's a lack of talent that discourages you and sometimes your tastes and interests just change as time passes. Whatever the reason, if you're no longer pursuing a hobby, you no longer need all the stuff associated with it.

If you once thought that embroidery was worth investigating, then discovered that you had absolutely no aptitude for it, why hang onto the hoops, the thread, the patterns, and the pile of fabric? If you took up guitar and then concluded that you had a tin ear, why keep it and the stacks of music and instruction books stashed in the back of your closet? If you used to have a passion for gardening, but have found now that you manage to kill just about everything you plant because you neglect it, why hide the tools, the gloves, the seed packets, and the gardening magazines in your garage?

Sometimes we keep this kind of stuff around for so long that it literally becomes invisible to us. It's well concealed somewhere out of the way, or, even if it's an everyday annoyance, we just get accustomed to pushing past it or working around it. Then one day, perhaps as we're unloading bunches of other things, it finally comes to our attention again. That's the time to grab it fast and toss it.

In some cases it could be that we hold onto the stuff associated with old hobbies because we feel that if we let it go, we've admitted some kind of terrible personal failure. Not true. No one is gifted or capable in all areas of life. Maybe you just need to keep searching for your special area.

Also, sometimes a person's interest in an activity is just not sustained for an entire lifetime. That's legitimate, too. It really doesn't matter how you felt in the past; all that matters is how you feel about the hobby now. If you're done with it, it's time to let all the old stuff go. Pass it along to someone who will be delighted to have it and then go off and find something brand new to do that brings you joy. Just stay alert to the amount of related things that you start to accumulate so that your new hobby doesn't end up becoming a huge stuff albatross.

* * * * *

TRUE CONFESSIONS: MAKING ART, MAKING A MESS

As I have mentioned, I'm an artist. It's a wonderful and challenging pastime that can be immensely satisfying on a personal level while at the same time completely devastating to any attempt at order in our home. I draw, paint and make hand-colored photographs on a regular basis, but I love all types of art and always want to experiment with different kinds of media. The Writer has commented that if there were any way that I could set up a welding shop, a ceramics kiln and a glass-blowing furnace in the confines of our home, I'd probably do it. He's right!

All the stuff associated with making art that I do keep around the house has on numerous occasions exploded into just about every corner of our living space. That kind of total disarray can cause plenty of frustrations and many delays while hunting for misplaced things. Eventually, it also can put a definite damper on one's enthusiasm. The annoyance caused to one's ever-suffering partner can only be imagined. Thankfully, the Writer has never felt compelled to verbalize it for my benefit, probably in part because he often has his own stuff scattered around the place, too.

Finally I had to acknowledge that my only hope to keep things under control was to edit the stuff down to the minimum that I need to be happy. As usual, it turned out to be far less than I had thought. When I appraised the situation honestly, it was clear that I was overloaded with all kinds of extra supplies. Some, like paint, had a limited shelf life; others, like a substantial pile of picture frames, were just too unwieldy to store easily.

So I decided to donate a bunch of the stuff overflow to an appropriate charity. What good are art supplies that never get made into art? I also try to remember that there are several well-stocked art supply stores nearby that serve quite admirably as my "storerooms." Just like the office supply stores, it's easier for me to let the merchants keep all of the stuff and then get the small quantity that I'm going to use when I'm actually ready to use it.

I also had to rethink some of my working habits. First, I had to narrow my focus so that I wasn't trying to make eleven different types of art at the same time, with the loads of stuff required for each project spread out all over. I think a lot of creative people suffer as I do from what I call "distractability." (No, I'm not referring to the condition called Attention Deficit Disorder; I think we are just very enthusiastic about multiple creative projects.) We have the tendency to get pulled from task to task because first one thing seems important, then another thing seems to warrant just as much immediate attention.

We start working on one project, get part way through developing it, then get excited about another idea and pull out all the necessary stuff to work on it. But we don't completely abandon the first thing that we started because it's still interesting. Instead, we try to keep both projects moving forward simultaneously because they're both interesting to us. If we do this a few more times, which is common, chaos is the certain outcome. Cutting way back on the "current projects" list is the only solution for me.

Next, I had to learn to discipline myself to put away things when I was done working with them. Even if I successfully stay focused on only one project and see it through to completion, I have a tendency to fall down on the follow-through of cleaning up. It's not because I'm lazy about putting things back (honest!); usually it's just because I'm always ready to leap onto the next project and don't want to lose momentum. But, again, that means that ultimately I lose lots of momentum when I have to deal with the inevitable confusion that results.

Although the rational part of my mind understands and accepts all of this, at times I still struggle mightily with these required changes in my old habits. It seems that my creative right brain prefers to remain an undisciplined child. But with time I have improved and I continue to try to make the best decisions that I can. For instance, just the other day the Writer was quite pleased to learn that I have abandoned my desire to take up life-size figure sculpting in concrete. At least for now.

* * * * *

TRUE CONFESSIONS: KID WISDOM

"Our son's position is to get rid of everything he isn't sure he'll need and want soon, which he thinks – as I do – is a reaction to the clutter of his parents. He was never a truly messy kid – you could always get into his room. But he says it wasn't until he went to boarding school that he consolidated his position, partly out of a desire to live in tidy surroundings and mostly so he could find things when he needed them for school, including clothes, papers, books, sports equipment. He didn't have time to search. He can't believe we don't get rid of our accumulation and more than once has volunteered to help with – or take over completely, since we don't seem to be able to do it ourselves – a serious thinning of our collection.

"Here's the kind of bind we face all the time. He has a beautiful four poster bed in his bedroom, which his father and I picked out for him a few years ago. He doesn't want it any more. He wants a simple, single, platform bed in a corner so he can have space for other things he wants in his room – a table for his computer, an easy chair and lamp. He wants us to sell the four poster at a garage sale we have planned since there's no place in the house to use it and no place to store it. His father wants to keep it (somewhere) because he really likes it and it would be great for guests if we ever build another room on the house!"

A Stuff-laden Friend

"Many possessions, if they do not make a man better, are at least expected to make his children happier, and this pathetic hope is behind many exertions."

George Santayana
1863-1952
The Life of Reason

KID CHAOS

Take a glance around any house in which there's a growing family and you're bound to see that kid stuff can be just as much of a problem as adult stuff. The only difference is that kids aren't to blame for accumulating all those things. Sorry, adults, but we're the ones who make the decisions when it comes to how much stuff children have, so we're the ones who need to take responsibility for getting things under control. Since this is another area in which I can claim no personal expertise, I did a little research. I also asked for suggestions from several friends who have managed to raise children and maintain their own sanity. Their kids seem to be turning out all right, too, so I assume that these parents must know something. And finally, I remembered how things were handled in my own family when I was growing up. Here is what I learned.

There are a couple of areas in which kid stuff can be a major problem. First, and most obvious, is keeping the number of toys and games under control. The most helpful thing adults can do for the children in their lives is to set a good example by not accumulating tons of their own stuff. Since many of us already have blown the opportunity to be a great role model in that particular area, the next best thing is to get the kids involved in your current household un-cluttering efforts. It's a great way to teach some values and share some family time while you're getting your home un-stuffed.

Working together is the perfect occasion to explain to your kids about the many other families who don't share your good fortune and how you can help them by donating some of your old stuff. Once they're aware that there are other children who don't have nice toys and games, most kids will respond to that information with complete understanding and will be willing to pass along some of their things. Then it's important to let them choose which ones they want to let go, although you might be surprised, or sometimes horrified, by their choices. Remember that you can't judge another person's stuff, even if the other person is a child.

Some families use an annual toy and game give-away system that helps them keep their kids' stuff from taking over their homes.

Every year around Thanksgiving, appropriately enough, the kids pull out all the playthings that have lost their charm. The worn out ones get tossed and the still usable ones are donated nice and early to one of the many charity holiday toy drives. Kids are usually very willing to participate in this ritual since they know that new holiday goodies are undoubtedly on their way to replace the old stuff.

Kids generally are not inclined to preserve their toys forever. It usually takes an adult mind to decide to buy something fabulous and then never touch it for fear of doing some kind of damage to it. The exceptions are those kids who decide at an early age to become collectors. If your child fits into that category, your job will be to make certain that there is a clear understanding of the difference between a collection and a whole bunch of stuff. Most little collectors, though, are quite savvy about collecting and know exactly what they like and why they like it. In that case, your pocketbook will determine just how elaborate your child's collection will become.

But for most kids, toys are there to be played with so it's no surprise when they eventually get outgrown, worn out or even completely destroyed. When kids grow tired of their stuff, for whatever reason, they rarely have any attachment to it, so it's easy for them to let it go. There's no guilt about who gave it to them, or concern if it hasn't been played with enough, or a desire simply to hold onto it as a keepsake. If it was a successful toy or game, it's been well used; if it's no longer useful, or if it never really was useful to them, it's not a problem to part with it. It would be so helpful to many of us adults if we adopted that very sensible way of looking at things and applied it when we were making decisions about our own stuff.

For the future, it's crucial to enlist the cooperation of family members and friends by making it known that toys or games are not your first choice for gifts. This will cause some consternation, but if you offer alternatives, that should make their decisions easier. Heaven help the poor adult who gives a kid something practical, so it's important to be creative. Gifts that encourage a child's interests in sports, music, reading, or art are usually on the "okay" list. And probably more than anything else, kids appreciate some undivided attention, so a day at an amusement park, or a bowling alley, or the professional ice skating show, for example, could be a great gift – as long as the kids don't come home laden with mounds of souvenirs.

Of course, all of us also must curb our own instincts to buy tons of toys for the kids in our lives, even if there's a lot of whining and crying going on. Parents or non-parents, everyone understands that saying no is a legitimate part of raising kids.

But the kids don't have to worry. There are still going to be plenty of toys and games around the house even if everyone does their best to cut back at least a bit on the quantity of the new stuff. No one is advocating complete toy and game abstinence. So the next issue that must be addressed is storage.

After you and your kids have purged all the unwanted items, and after you've sorted and gathered the remainder of the kid stuff, it's time to think about containers. Durability, flexibility, and ease of use for the kids are the criteria to look for when you're figuring out storage. Get creative with old furniture and boxes or check out the scads of stores and catalogues devoted to storage ideas. If all the toys and games have a place to be put away, at least you stand a fighting chance that they will be. "Fighting" is the operative word here, because you'll still have to struggle to get most kids to stop playing long enough to clean up and put away everything they have spread out all over the place. Just think of it as another opportunity for character building – yours.

The second major area in which kid stuff can get out of hand concerns school papers and artistic projects. I think the most helpful idea I learned about handling these items is to let each child have one good-sized box that will be devoted to holding everything for the entire year. That way you can also include things like items made at summer camp or drawings done while on the family vacation. Special things might be displayed for awhile, but then they would go into the box.

Right before the next school year begins, you and your child go through the box together and pick out the items that the child wants to save. Again, it's important to let the child choose what to keep. Don't be surprised if it's less than you want to hang onto. You can add a few of your own choices, too, if you think something genuinely important has been overlooked. But do your best not to get stuck in the Sentimental Trap; remember that this is supposed to be a time for eliminating things. That way you're keeping only the exceptional papers and projects created by your exceptional child. This will help your child (and you) get into the habit of throwing away the unwanted stuff before it turns into piles of trouble in the future.

For the next year, you start a new box. After a few years, you can go through everything in each of the boxes with your child. You'll discover that some items have lost their luster, so you can sort again to decide on the best things that you both still want to keep. Then you'll be able to consolidate several years into one box and you won't continue to store a lot of unnecessary stuff. Use this system all through the school years to keep kid stuff under control. When your kids grow up, they'll be delighted to have a couple of boxes of prized mementos of their schooldays. And, with any luck, you will have taught them a good way to handle stuff when they have kids of their own.

* * * * *

Clutter can be very stressful for the adults who live in the middle of it, but it can also have an unfortunate psychological effect on the kids in the home. Some young children can become disturbed and agitated by the chaos in their cluttered rooms and over-stuffed houses, but they usually have no clear awareness of the connection between their feelings and their surroundings.

Older kids who don't like the clutter can be negatively affected, too, if it interferes with a place for them to study or if they're frustrated in what they would like to do because their disorganized rooms lack storage. If the situation is truly out of control, they might even be too embarrassed to bring friends to their homes. Also, just because your kids seem to be totally oblivious to the mess around them and often seem to do more than their share of contributing to it, don't assume that they don't care about it. You could discover that just the opposite is true.

Now, obviously, a loving family can make up for a whole lot of chaos in the home, but why allow a bunch of stuff to get in the way of your kids' peace of mind? If you have children who might be affected by your clutter, there could hardly be an easier choice: unimportant stuff or very important kids?

So, once you've cleared out all of the unnecessary things and straightened up the place, it's likely that you'll find your kids are delighted with their new orderly environment. It also helps children get a sense of security when they're not confronted with confusion all around them at home. There's enough chaos and confusion that they have to face when they go out there into the world. When your home is a calmer place, your kids may seem calmer, too. Since you'll also be more relaxed and happier, your relationship with your children might even improve a notch or two. That's a significant win/win situation, just from un-stuffing your life.

* * * * *

TIDBIT: THE USEFUL BOX

By the way, the box-it-up method of storing your kids' schoolwork is an excellent way to handle adult stuff, too. If you have one box where you toss all of your potential "keeper stuff" for a year, and then you sort through it annually, you can stay very well organized. Making the commitment to do this every year would be required, but that ought to be manageable even for the most paper-phobic among us, like me. It's definitely a better approach than spending all your free time going through decades of unsorted stuff later in life.

* * * * *

TRUE CONFESSIONS: MY CHILDHOOD COLLECTION

When I was a child, I became a collector of miniature animal figures. My organized mother thoughtfully set up a small bookcase in my bedroom for me to display my growing collection, which encompassed everything from delicate glass swans to ceramic giraffes to detailed cast metal dogs, none more than about an inch or two high. I was quite proud of it and took full responsibility for regularly dusting each tiny figure.

I don't remember if I lost interest or if I just ran out of room on my shelves and Mom called a halt to adding any more little animals, but when I got older eventually I did stop collecting. However, I didn't hand off the collection to anyone else or donate it or try to sell it. Instead I headed off to college and my hundred-or-so tiny creatures headed into in a cardboard box, stashed in my parents' basement. When they moved and no longer had room for all of my stuff, they sent the box (among others) to me. Then I ended up storing it and hauling it around from place to place for years and years.

I report with great chagrin that I am only now photographing the collection so that I can list it in an on-line auction. I've finally escaped from The Sentimental Trap.

Well, okay, maybe I'll just keep two or three of the little ones that I still particularly like . . .

* * * * *

MY STORY: THE STUFFED GARAGE

The pressures of cleaning out stuff had just about become unbearable when I made the brilliant decision to tackle the storeroom in the back of our garage. Actually, the Writer made the decision and I was dragged along kicking and screaming. Apparently he had decided that renting a storeroom in addition to the storeroom we already had at home was no longer justifiable now that we were "downsizing," as some people politely call the de-junking process.

We had downsized quite literally just a few years back when we moved from a large house into a much smaller townhouse. Unfortunately, we didn't downsize most of our stuff prior to making the move. As a result, and at no small expense, three burly movers carted massive amounts of furniture and boxes of things into our much smaller abode. The substantial overflow went into the rental storage unit.

Looking back, I see now that it would have been far more sensible to dispose of all the furniture and the dishes and decorative stuff prior to moving. Instead, the burly movers got a hearty workout, on our nickel, hauling tons of stuff that had now been sold or given away or trashed. But, as we well know, sensible thinking often does not prevail when it comes to the process of unloading one's things.

And now the Writer wanted to unload the storeroom. Obviously, one cannot simply cram an entire storeroom's worth of items into another storeroom that is already fully crammed. However, he explained to me patiently, if we reorganized the garage storeroom first, then we could fit everything from the rental storage unit into it, finally bringing all of our possessions under one roof again.

I don't know what happened to cause the Writer to become so enthusiastic about getting rid of stuff, but for several months he had been approaching the task with impressive zeal. I claim for myself only a modicum of praise as the source of his inspiration. I'm more inclined to believe that he sprang into action when the sheer quantity of stuff surrounding him finally reached some kind of critical mass in his brain and tipped him over the edge. Whatever the case, the kind of fervor he exhibited was very motivating for me to overcome my struggles with the process. And it was certainly helpful in the overall effort to un-clutter the household.

People who lack un-cluttering support in their own home regrettably have an additional emotional burden to bear, not to mention lots of additional stuff that can't be touched. Other household residents who seem to be indifferent usually become surprisingly protective of their own things. If they are openly hostile, their efforts to maintain the status quo could turn the process into a full-scale battle. And one does not necessarily want to draw battle lines that might jeopardize an entire relationship just because a complete collection of *Star Wars* lunch boxes and Aunt Lucinda's scruffy armoire are constantly in the way. On the other hand . . . well, that sort of decision must be made on a case-by-case basis.

In our case, I initially expressed utter horror at the mere thought of trying to accomplish the monumental feat of vacating the storeroom. I believe I may have even cried out something rather unkind regarding the Writer's sanity. For weeks, he had been trekking over to the storeroom, bringing home a box or two at a time and dealing with the contents. This seemed manageable. But impatience got the best of him and he wanted everything here, now.

Eventually I was won over by his strong convictions and the sobering realization that he would implement his plan with or without my cooperation. So I joined him in moving out the cars, then standing in the middle of our garage to peruse the situation.

Our garage is lined on all three usable walls with shelving. The Writer had neatly arranged various items and boxes on each of the shelves and had carefully stacked boxes of more stuff under the stairs. The garage was his domain, so most of the contents belonged to him. The place was packed.

Some of the boxes were full of things he once had considered useful, such as postal shipping materials (handy for e-Bay) and numerous computer-related items. There were rows of videotapes on the shelves and his business art files that were too large for a filing cabinet. There were also several boxes of my artwork and a stack of empty frames for future use. The other detritus of life, such as picnic baskets and ice chests, garden tools and paint cans, a small hand-held car vacuum, a couple of quarts of oil, were scattered amongst the boxes. He had already worked hard to get the place in this shape. It appeared crowded but mostly under control. I would have been content to let it be and have him slowly continue the piecemeal unloading of stuff. The thought of adding everything from the rental storeroom into the mix all at once was completely incomprehensible to me.

The Writer looked over the stacks and shelves, nodded and muttered to himself. I stood silently next to him, watching closely and wondering if I should have him committed. I quickly dismissed the idea and vowed to be fully supportive of his plan, no matter how extreme it might be.

Moments later, we stepped into the storeroom behind the area where the cars are usually parked to examine it. It, too, was full of various boxes (his), unpainted canvasses (mine), Christmas decorations (ours). However, it was far less orderly in appearance. In one corner I spotted a stack of boxes that I knew belonged to me. The Writer glanced around briefly, then announced that fitting everything in here would require both of us to sort through and toss out a lot of this other stuff to make room. This simple and reasonable declaration caused me to gasp aloud.

"But some of these boxes in here are my family things! Stuff from my childhood! My entire life history! How can I get rid of any of it?!" I fairly reeled in shock at the mere idea.

"At least look at it. If you want to keep it, then you have to find stuff somewhere else that's easier to let go," he replied calmly. "I'm going to have to do the same thing, you know."

I don't know why, but it seems that we can always readily spot the trashable items that belong to others even though we have great difficulty with our own stuff. I gestured toward one overflowing box belonging to him. "You could toss those old magazines," I volunteered, rather helpfully I thought.

The Writer winced slightly. "Thank you so much for pointing that out," he said with a distinct lack of genuine gratitude. "Why don't we each just stick to dealing with our own stuff?"

"Okay," I agreed, a bit downcast. Then I grudgingly selected a box for him to carry upstairs for me to go through. This was not going to be easy. The fact that he had his own difficult decisions ahead of him, I confess, did not engender much sympathy at that particular moment.

Since I had already survived the trauma of finally selling the family antique furniture (alas, no room) and had sold or given away lots of the dishes and decorative stuff (alas, again, no room), I was mostly down to the really, really personal items. Resigned to the task and hoping I could survive this trauma, too, I opened the first box with great trepidation.

Yearbooks. I couldn't possibly toss away my school history. Thankfully, I recalled that our most recent book purge had cleared enough space on a bookcase for them. My master's thesis. I couldn't toss that. There was still blood on the pages. I found a small box full of childhood mementos, souvenirs from my first train trip with my mother and a few pieces of dime-store jewelry from a favorite Halloween costume. A scrapbook from my grandparents' 50th anniversary party. My first "published" story, included as part of a collection of stories and poems written by selected junior high English scholars and distributed, to our delight, to the entire school.

The sorting process dragged on for several weeks. The Writer slogged almost daily through the mounds of stuff down in the garage. He tossed, he re-packed, he shoved boxes around. He seriously considered the virtues of selling versus donating and vice versa. Piles moved back and forth between the two categories, often several times, depending on his mood. He hauled tons of paper to the recycling center. He gave away outdated videos. He trashed obsolete computer software and equipment while railing against their stupendous loss of value. In fact, I occasionally observed him speaking harshly to a number of inanimate objects as he worked. Most of the time he was positively brutal when making decisions about what to keep and what to toss. It was breathtaking. I could see empty space on the shelves.

Upstairs, I was moving much more slowly. I had surprisingly little desire to examine the contents of my comparatively small number of designated boxes, even though the memories they evoked were uniformly pleasant. As I reluctantly worked my way through this very personal stuff, I realized that the most difficult part of the task was that after the joy of discovery and remembering, my head sort of felt stuck in the past. Of course, the past was at the core of the entire sorting and tossing process, and I had felt stuck there before. But the stuff of one's personal history is some of the most emotion-laden stuff one can confront. And after all the things I had already sorted through, I was now completely at odds with what I was doing, wanting very much to live in the moment or at least be thinking of the future rather than the past. Even the happiest memories began to feel slightly debilitating. I decided that this was irrefutable proof of how important it is to keep up with organizing stuff regularly instead of having to do it many years later when it would be much nicer just to enjoy having it.

This difficult task proved to be an important one, however, because I discovered some treasured items that desperately needed to be rescued. There were important newspaper clippings that were almost disintegrating. There were Polaroid photos that were on the verge of totally losing their images. In one, my childhood tennis partner and I sadly had been reduced to faded reddish-brown blobs atop four scrawny legs. Thank Heaven for computers and scanners; at least I would salvage what I could. There were a few things that hadn't survived the years at all and required disposal with unceremonious haste, most tragically a few well-loved stuffed animals that had developed an odor we decided was borderline toxic.

Ultimately, I found that I simply repacked most of the items. There weren't all that many boxes left after I had done a little bit of consolidating and organizing. I decided that was okay. It was my life history, after all, so condensing it to a few boxes didn't seem too outlandish. And someday in the distant future, when I was in just the right frame of mind, I would go through the boxes again and be happy that I had kept all those wonderful mementos. Or maybe by then I'd even be ready to let more of them go.

Days later, another set of unsuspecting burly movers carted over the final load of the most incredibly heavy boxes from the rental storeroom. Our garage and its back room were completely packed again, with barely enough space left for the cars. But everything was all there, under one roof. The Writer felt positively triumphant. I was pleased, too, and felt no small amount of admiration for the success of his efforts. We proudly surveyed the entire crowded area together.

"There's still a lot to go through," he observed. "But at least it's all accessible."

"I'm glad you saved room for my boxes," I said gratefully. The Writer had his arm over my shoulder and he gave me a little squeeze. "I have a few more in the hall closet that I'd like to bring down here, too," I added.

"Really?" The Writer seemed surprised. "But we're all jammed up again. Where could they go?"

"Well, you still could get rid of that pile of magazines, or that box over there . . . " I helpfully began to suggest a few possibilities that were obvious to me.

The silence was deafening.

* * * * *

TIDBIT: STASHED IN STORAGE

What exactly is in your storage unit? You've got twenty, forty, maybe even a hundred square feet of space and it's packed to the rafters. You pay a decent amount of money for it every month, money that you could use for other things like the rent, or the car payment, or braces for your youngest. You might use that money to go out to a nice restaurant once in awhile, or maybe you'd save up and remodel the kitchen, or even better, take a vacation. But instead, you're paying for a home for your stuff.

Old papers, old appliances, old furniture, old clothes, and boxes of all kinds of mysterious items are requiring you to work, probably at least for an extra hour or two every month, just so that they can sit comfortably in storage. Sure, you realize that it's extra money spent, but what about that extra time you spend working? Is there some other way you might like to use that?

And what about the time spent just thinking about your storeroom full of stuff? You're always aware of it and you know that you'll need to do something about it someday. Sometimes you wonder if you'll ever actually get around to using any of those old things. Then you wonder if everything's okay, and worry that there might have been a fire or a flood or a break in. What if the storeroom has termites? There goes Aunt Agatha's chest of drawers.

Even though we might talk about "disposable income," I don't know of anyone who wants to pour hard-earned wages down the drain. And I don't think I've ever met any people who say that they have time to spare. So how much time and money do you waste on storing your old stuff?

* * * * *

"All my possessions for a moment of time."

Elizabeth I
1533-1603
Attributed as her final words.

UN-STUFFING WHILE YOU STILL CAN

One of the primary reasons that we avoid dealing with all of our stuff and things is that we believe that we are immortal. Well, maybe we really do know that we aren't, but we have an awfully hard time coming to grips with the fact that someday there is an end to the road ahead. Instead we pretend that we're going to live forever, so we just keep on accumulating all kinds of excess stuff along the way. Unfortunately, that means that not only do we haul our huge loads of stuff around with us throughout our lives, but then we leave it behind for our nearest and dearest to deal with once we've left this mortal realm. Yes, it is true that you can't take it with you.

Of course, sometimes an inheritance is a wonderful gift. It's safe to assume valuable antiques and fine art will be appreciated, even if only because they are easily saleable. A nice bank account undoubtedly will be received gratefully, as will some very personal items that have special meaning for the recipient. But leaving behind all of our junk and clutter for our heirs to sort through surely is not the ideal way to say good-bye. When that happens, the heirs are left coping with their grief plus dealing with our childhood collection of soda bottle caps; the beat-up old lawn furniture in the basement; a closet full of sales samples from the job we used to have fifteen years ago; and all the rest of the useless stuff that, for some reason, we couldn't seem to let go.

The unhappy heirs usually don't have a clue about how we would have liked for them to handle the raft of things that they now face. Most probably they also have to get past the sort of squeamish feeling that they're invading our privacy in ways they would have preferred to avoid. And this presumes that everybody is getting along fine and cooperating in the estate settling process. How often have we heard of families, or experienced the situation ourselves, in which just the opposite happened? Many of us already know the difficulties that can arise between family members because each of them has a different idea about how to distribute the "good stuff" and dispose of the rest.

Often the biggest problem results from family members wanting the same item, causing some pretty nasty squabbles. And the fights aren't necessarily over anything that has monetary value. Certain things just trigger sentimental attachments that get our feelings stirred up right at a time when we're already about as stirred up as we can get. "Mom would have wanted me to have the souvenir ashtray from the campgrounds because I loved camping more than you did." "You weren't even on the trip when we got that ashtray, but I was, so I think I should have it." "Look, I'm the oldest so I think I'm the one who should decide." And so on.

It's a sad situation when the passing of a person's life is marked primarily by family hostilities. Those bad feelings can last all through the laborious days of sorting out a fully packed home. That experience is already stressful enough, since it's likely that everyone will be rushed trying to complete the difficult process. Top that off with further emotional bruises from another month's worth of weekend garage sales. In the process, some family members stop speaking to each other. Joint vacation plans and holiday dinners are cancelled. Meanwhile, sensible young kids are left wondering why everyone else seems so angry when they're just feeling sad because a loved one is gone. A time when everyone should be pulling together ends up being a time when some families get pulled apart. And all of this turmoil is caused by the stuff we left behind.

If the specter of a family disaster isn't enough to motivate some of us to de-junk and un-clutter now, maybe a little ego-gratification for our controlling natures will get us going. If you've already prepared a will or a trust document, you're well on your way to making certain that your estate is handled the way you want it to be when you're no longer around. But even the most detailed wills and trusts rarely deal with every single piece of stuff you own. So if you want to have a definite say in how things are distributed, some distributing in advance is a good way to go. It's also a good way to find out if anyone actually is interested in all the stuff that you think is so special. You may be in for a few surprises because there's no guarantee that the other members of your family are going to be as enthusiastic as you are about those things. You might as well know right now exactly how they feel so that you don't spend your entire life hanging onto Uncle Finster's hockey puck collection when nobody else wants it.

Another thing that you might want to consider is leaving a list of smaller household and personal items in your file with your will or trust in which you specify who will inherit what when the time comes. It's much nicer for the family if your list states clearly that Junior is the one who gets the campgrounds ashtray but his siblings also have personal items designated for them. That way, you've done your best to prevent any arguing that otherwise might have come up. And if there are still disputes in spite of your fine efforts, at least you won't have to deal with them!

As I've already mentioned, I sometimes jokingly refer to my un-stuffing efforts as my "pre-estate sale." But it really isn't much of a joke. The truth is that I like to think that I've been a good caretaker for the things that I'm handing off and I try to remember that caretaking is really all that any of us are doing for our stuff. So, all the "good stuff" that I'm not using and enjoying, I'm giving to family and friends or selling; all the remaining excess stuff I'm tossing or donating. It's simplifying my life, it makes the new caretakers happy, and it's generating some cash that I can use on things that play an active role in my life now rather than things that just don't work for me anymore.

I also try to remember that letting go of our stuff, especially much of our sentimental stuff, is an ongoing process. It takes time, not just time to sort and dispose of items, but time to reflect on the meaning behind them. Taking that time will allow us to discover gradually that we need much less than we think we do to be happy.

* * * * *

TRUE CONFESSIONS: PARENTS' STUFF

Lark's mother recently passed away after a long illness. She had lived in the same house for almost forty years and her two adult children inherited the place. It was packed with all the usual household stuff plus an enormous collection of family memorabilia. In the midst of the massive sorting and tossing project that followed, my exhausted friend remarked, "There's nothing like having to shut down a parent's house and deal with all of their stuff to make you realize that you can't take it with you."

* * * * *

Madelaine can't even comprehend why her aging mother refuses to pare down the incredible amount of stuff that fills her home, which is hours away from Maddy. And her mom has a penchant for stashing her valuables in secret places without bothering to share the specifics with her daughter. What happens when mom is gone? Maddy doesn't even want to think about it, but we know an already difficult situation will be made even more difficult by all that stuff.

* * * * *

Leeanne's elderly parents both had to be moved to an assisted living facility, leaving my friend and her siblings with the huge task of clearing out a packed-to-the-rafters house that needed to be sold quickly. Her comment: "People should remember that there's no U-Haul at the back of the hearse."

* * * * *

BUYING NEW STUFF

Even if we're dutifully paring down to the bare essentials of life, eventually we must face up to purchasing new items. If we're committed to keeping our lives uncomplicated by lots of excess stuff, buying something new might even be a bit nerve wracking. We don't want to contribute to more clutter in our homes, but we do need to be able to function in the world. Occasionally, we might even want to be indulgent and allow ourselves a luxury item. This is supposed to be a joyful life, after all, not punishment for a crime.

When you're thinking of buying something new, there are really only three criteria you need in order to determine if it's a good idea to go ahead with the purchase. It doesn't matter if you're buying a luxury item or purchasing something completely mundane, the criteria are the same:

Function: Does this item serve some purpose? Do you need it to get through your day? Will it help you be more productive? ("My husband needs some shaving cream. I'll pick some up for him.") Knowing that the thing will be used is the single most significant factor.

Aesthetic Appeal: Do you simply love what you see? Is it so wonderful that you can't imagine living without it? ("Wow! Look at this incredibly gorgeous shaving brush and antique cup to hold the cream! He would love it!") Getting something that you like makes sense, but getting something that you adore is even better.

Price: Can you afford it? Are you willing to work extra hours if you need extra cash to pay for it? Are you willing to give up that time in order to have it? ("Uh-oh. Check the price. Well, maybe for his birthday . . .") Unless your income level is stratospheric, price is always an issue. But it's also important to remember that price alone is not a reason to buy anything. Just because you can afford it or even because you think it's a terrific deal doesn't make buying something a good idea. Ten cases of canned tuna may be a bargain, but if you don't have a place to put them, the hassle pretty much negates the money you would save. And we already know that the concept of disposable income doesn't mean that it's okay to waste any extra cash you might be lucky enough to have.

Remember that when you're thinking about buying something new, it needs to have a legitimate purpose, whether it's utilitarian or aesthetic. This is a good time to refer to that helpful inventory list that you made when you started your big un-cluttering job. If an item doesn't qualify to go on the list, it's time to rethink the purchase. Preferably before you buy it.

* * * * *

TIDBIT: QUANTITY

What would you rather have: lots of stuff or a few really nice things?

What would you rather have: lots of luxurious stuff or the luxury of time?

* * * * *

TIDBIT: QUALITY

When buying new, think quality, not quantity. One day when I was purchasing a nice handbag, the young salesgirl helping me commented that she wished that she could afford to buy one for herself. I asked her how many handbags she owned and, after some thought, she decided she probably had at least six. When we added together the cost of each of her less expensive bags, the total exceeded the cost of the one nice, very versatile bag that she really wanted. Maybe one really good item is a better buy than lots of just okay items. And it's a sure way to own less stuff.

* * * * *

TIDBIT: COLLECTING

True collectors are usually enthusiastic people who adore their collections and are eager to share their excitement about them with others. They make sure that their collections are well cared for and displayed in a way that maximizes the enjoyment of everyone who sees them.

I'm convinced that people who already have too much stuff should avoid collecting anything, at least until their stuff situation is under control. Otherwise, it's too easy to end up with a whole lot of things rather than a real collection.

So let's think of the decision not to collect anything as choosing to go on a kind of healthy diet, except in this case you're helping out your mental health. If you go on a diet to lose weight, you probably don't like to keep lots of fattening foods around the house to tempt you. You might even try to avoid the candy and bakery aisles when you go to the grocery store.

The same is true of collecting. Once you get started, you want to add more and more to your collection. That means shopping. Shopping means putting yourself in dangerous environments like malls or antique shops or online auctions where you're surrounded by stuff. Why tempt yourself with all kinds of things just to add more stuff to your collection?

* * * * *

TIDBIT: OWNERSHIP

Do you really need to own everything that you like? Can you appreciate something without owning it? Try thinking of your favorite home furnishings store or boutique that sells decorative stuff or collectibles shop as a museum. Let them own the "collection." You can just visit occasionally and enjoy looking at it!

* * * * *

DECORATING AND STUFF

I admit that I got hooked on many of the home design and decorating shows that proliferate on television. I confess that I have also frequently succumbed to the urge to purchase "shelter magazines" – you know the ones with the highly paid, highly fashionable interior designers showing off their latest efforts, usually in some unbelievably spectacular mansions.

But I've finally managed to regain some control of myself. It wasn't too difficult once I acknowledged that the primary purpose for these TV shows and glossy magazines was to advocate the accumulation of more stuff. Yes, there were a few minimalist designers who were featured and the occasional program devoted to some fairly spartan loft living, but in most cases, the message was clear: buy more, buy more, buy more.

There seemed to be an inevitable need for more color, more pattern, more texture everywhere. Every inch of wall space was considered incomplete until it was filled with or covered by something. Every available surface was a candidate for artfully arranged displays of one's possessions. The decorators always suggested ways for one's stuff to make a greater "impact." In our cluttered situations, more impact from our stuff is exactly what we're trying to avoid! And yet I heard allegedly respected designers and enthusiastic amateurs alike exclaim fervently, "Too much is never enough!"

This is downright horrifying to someone who suffers from Stuff Attacks. I know that personal tastes vary greatly when it comes to decorating and I'm all for expressing individual style, but for many of us, any sense of style has been all but lost in the general chaos that surrounds us. If one's home reflects one's inner state of being, there's a whole lot of turmoil going on in a whole lot of heads.

I don't know what prompts the urge to fill empty space, but I think it's worthwhile to resist it. For many of us, it's absolutely necessary to resist it because if we don't, we end up feeling overwhelmed or claustrophobic or constantly agitated. If there's nowhere for the eye to rest, the brain doesn't get a break either.

One of the most productive things that we can do that will protect us from stuff overload in the future is to get comfortable with emptiness. Empty walls don't always need to be plastered with pictures and sconces and dried flower wreaths, or even covered with decorative paint treatments. Bare tables can be quite attractive all by themselves. A single rose in a bud vase can be a beautiful vision as readily as a huge bouquet if it can be seen clearly rather than lost in a sea of clutter.

When we're considering the furnishings of our home, of course we want our rooms to be attractive and comfortable. But is there anything else we can agree on, no matter what our decorating style? Well, there's at least one thing. Space.

We know that we need enough space to accommodate our necessary things and ourselves comfortably. We don't want to be tripping over the ottoman and bumping into the bookcase every time we walk through a room. I once saw a home decorating television show in which the host explained that it was important to leave eighteen inches between the furniture and coffee table. Do you realize what a tiny amount of space eighteen inches is? He also left the same amount of space between the various other huge pieces of furniture in the jam-packed room. This made it impossible to navigate the area without constantly doing a little dance between obstacles. I'd rather do my dancing on a dance floor and be able to move easily and freely throughout my home.

We also need to have enough space to display our special items in such a way that they can be enjoyed. Unless we are able continually to relocate to bigger quarters, the only way for most of us to get enough space is to keep our inventory list of what we need as small as possible and keep the excess stuff totally out of our lives.

In some traditional Japanese homes, there is an area defined as a place of honor in which only special objects are displayed, often as few as one or two harmonious items such as a hanging scroll and a flower arrangement. That way their full beauty can be appreciated without distractions. The objects are changed seasonally or for celebratory occasions. You may not want to subscribe to quite such an austere aesthetic, but if your home is packed to the rafters with stuff, can you really appreciate and enjoy all of it? Maybe rotating some of your favorite decorative stuff in and out of storage would allow it to command more attention. Or maybe if you pack some things away, you'll decide that you like the simplified look better and you can just let everything else go.

Of course, it's only sensible to avoid purchasing any new decorative things until the unloading of all the old excess stuff is complete, or at least nearly complete. Then, after you've done a terrific job of eliminating the stuff that you don't need, you'll be able to see what it was that attracted you to the items that you've kept, without a layer or two of extra things around to obscure them. It's possible that you might find your new, pared down style to be exactly what you want, just as it is. It's also possible that once you actually get a good look at what you have, you'll realize that you really don't like any of it anymore!

If you do decide to make any changes, as long as you stick to the guidelines you used to make up your inventory list, you should be able to make your new purchases without creating more problems for yourself. Just ask the basic questions and answer them honestly: Is it truly useful? Do I simply adore the way it looks? Can I really afford it? If the new item passes the test, you'll know that it's a worthwhile purchase.

* * * * *

TIDBIT: HOUSECLEANING

The primary benefit of unloading all your excess stuff is the enormous sense of relief and the feelings of freedom that result, not to mention the practical benefit of more space. But one of the nice fringe benefits of less stuff is that your home is so much easier to keep clean. No more lifting every little knick-knack, no more moving around stacks and piles of things, and no more frustration because even after spending hours cleaning it, the place never actually looks clean. Even if you have hired help to assist with the cleaning chores, this means that the job will take less time and, as a result, cost less money. A win/win situation!

* * * * *

'TIS BETTER TO GIVE THAN TO RECEIVE

Where do we get lots of our stuff? Much of it comes from other well-meaning people who give us gifts. It's hard to believe that such generosity could cause problems, but sometimes it does. Because of our over-developed sense of obligation to our stuff, once we get something, we have a hard time letting go of it. So even the most inappropriate gifts, or the gifts that just miss the mark, or the gifts that would be perfectly all right if we didn't have six of the same thing already, end up as stuff we hopelessly try to figure out how to use. Knowing how difficult it is for us to deal with stuff, surely we don't want to inflict the same problem on others by giving them gifts that end up as just more stuff in their lives. But how can that be avoided?

First, let's try to understand the psychology behind gift giving. Way back when we were kids, we learned all about the importance of giving presents to others. "We have to take a gift to the neighbor's party." "Let's get a gift for your teacher now that it's the end of the school year." "We always buy gifts for each other for the holidays." And so on. We understood at an early age that the gifts were supposed to be "nice things" that the person receiving them would like. You also might have learned that if someone really "cared," they would spend extra money on a gift. Get something bigger. Get something fancier. Get something more. "Charlie is your best friend. You should pick out something nicer for him."

There also were times when you discovered that giving a gift was an obligation rather than an expression of affection. "Do I really have to give Freddie a birthday present? I don't even like him." "Of course you have to give him a present! I'm on the charity committee at church with his mother."

Maybe there were occasions when you watched your parents choose expensive gifts just to impress other people. "This will show them how well we're doing!" And you probably saw someone purchase a gift in a rush. "Just get something! Anything! And have the store wrap it fast! We're running late!"

Whatever the occasion, whoever the recipient, whatever the depth of feeling involved, you knew that it was important to get some "thing," in most cases as a gesture of your friendship or your love.

It's no surprise that from all of these experiences, children easily could assume that the thing itself really is what counts, not the thought, as the adults inevitably liked to tell them.

Of course, most of the time we have the best of intentions (those dangerous things again) and we do want to give gifts that will be appreciated and enjoyed. But the familiar ritual of buying a "thing" easily can obscure the significance of the act of giving. What if we approached buying gifts in the same way that we now approach buying something new for ourselves, something we could add comfortably to our inventory list? What if we chose something that could be added to a similar inventory list that we imagine our friends or relatives might create?

A couple of years ago my mother bought us a new refrigerator as a gift. It was certainly going to be functional, it was much more attractive than the old one, and it fit her budget. We could not have been happier with her choice. She could have spent her money on lots of little things that we didn't really need or want, but that would have been less satisfying for everyone. The refrigerator was the perfect gift for us. And it could easily go on our inventory list.

There's probably something functional that you could think of for some of the people on your gift list. Obviously, it doesn't need to be an item as large as a refrigerator. When I moved into my very first apartment, one of my housewarming gifts from my parents was a small set of screwdrivers. I'm still using them today. You might choose a long coveted tool for the woodworker, a few cans of tennis balls for the sport lover, a set of watercolors for the budding artist. You really need to know your recipients well in order to make this work, otherwise you'll just be guessing and they'll end up with another thing that adds to their own problems with stuff. But it's guaranteed that if the gift will get used, it will be appreciated.

What if we thought about buying gifts that were not things at all, or at least were things that would get used up completely? Now that's a very attractive idea for the overburdened, stuff-laden people on your list, which is just about everyone. The possibilities are limited only by one's imagination. The obvious choices are flowers and candy; not many people would object to either or both as a gift. You can always make the gift a bit more special by choosing flowers from your own garden or making the candy yourself. In fact, homemade food of any kind is one of the most reliable gifts for showing appreciation or demonstrating how much you care about someone.

But there are many, many more choices. Tickets to the theater or a concert for your spouse. Tuition for the weaving class that your friend is eager to take. A gift certificate for a massage or a day at a spa for your stressed-out sister. A long distance phone card for your nephew who's away at school. Scented candles for your co-worker. Or, perhaps one of the best choices of all, your time.

If you have a particular skill, offering your time and services is a unique and meaningful gift. If you're handy around the house, help out with some painting or carpentry that needs to be done at the home of the lucky recipient. If you're a good photographer, take pictures of the new baby, the new house, or the family dog, and put them in an album. If you're a computer expert, spend some time explaining how to get that finicky new software to work properly.

All you need is a driver's license to offer regular rides to the grocery store for an older friend who has no transportation. If you're available to baby-sit, offer gift certificates of baby-sitting time to a young mom who could use a little time to herself. In fact, you could easily make up your own personal gift certificates for any of these ideas or others that are more appropriate for your needs.

We all know that the best gifts are not necessarily the most expensive ones. The best gifts are the ones that allow us to connect with each other in a meaningful way. It turns out that it really is the thought that counts. So, if you're terribly clever, and if you let it be known that you're trying to avoid accumulating any more stuff in your life, maybe you can inspire your friends and family with these ideas. Then they'll become more aware of the interesting options available to them when they're choosing gifts for you, too. Less stuff for them, less stuff for you. I love a happy ending!

TIDBIT: THE LOVELY GIFT

If you received a gift of flowers and their time has now passed, it's okay to throw away the vase or container along with the faded blossoms. It's okay to throw away the cute little decorative teddy bear on a plastic rod that was stuck in the side. And the balloon, too. It's even okay to throw away the gift card that came along.

Just keep the love.

* * * * *

TIDBIT: ABUNDANCE

It's wonderful to enjoy the abundance that life offers and quite appropriate to have gratitude for it. But that doesn't mean we're required to own an abundance of stuff in order to savor life. In fact, the greatest feeling of abundance comes when you can honestly say:

"I have enough."

* * * * *

THE UN-STUFFED LIFE

When you clear out your plentiful assortment of excess stuff and things, you not only straighten up your home, you also clear out space in your head. All that stuff isn't on your mind to torture you anymore. You know that you can use the cleaned out areas in your home more efficiently, but that brain space can be put to better use, too. Once your stuff burden has been lifted, you'll probably be surprised at how incredibly liberated you feel. That's the time to move on to examine another area that you may not have considered: unloading all the superfluous stuff in your life.

It isn't just a bunch of objects that can weigh you down and keep you from experiencing life to the fullest; there also can be other sources of excess baggage that probably will start to manifest themselves in ways you never noticed until you un-stuffed your home.

Do you have a job that you hate? Have you made commitments to participate in activities that now make you feel trapped? Do you have a friend who is constantly complaining and negative about everything? Maybe it's time to let go of these things, too.

It's okay to jettison people who have nothing to offer but cynicism and negativity. In fact, it's crucial to your own mental health. I'm not talking about a friend or relative who's going through an emotional rough spot; I'm referring to the kind of people we've all encountered who constantly wallow in misery and seem to be on a mission to bring other people down along with them.

You undoubtedly have plans and dreams and ideas that excite you, so doesn't it make more sense to surround yourself with people who are not only encouraging to you but also enthusiastic about their own lives? It's simply more stimulating – and more fun – to be around someone who has a positive attitude. Plus you have the added benefit of most probably learning a new thing or two from other people who are immersed in their own varied interests.

It's also fine to stop participating in the routine social and recreational commitments that no longer hold any appeal for you. If you've faithfully attended monthly meetings of a best-seller reading group that has turned into little more than a gossip-fest, this is probably the right time to bid them adieu. If you've always played golf every Sunday afternoon, but you'd really like to try tennis, why not skip the links and hit the courts? Maybe you were voted Acting Secretary of the garden club, just until they could find someone with more time to take on the job, but you've noticed that your "temporary" position has lasted several years. If you want to step aside so that you can squeeze in a few more hours to devote to actual gardening, that's a reasonable decision. Your time is a precious commodity that you don't want to squander. Somehow, quite miraculously of course, everyone will cope without your continued presence.

Since the majority of our day is usually occupied by work, most of us don't hesitate to re-evaluate our jobs if they become unsatisfying. Whether it's in an office or at home, whether it's paid employment or unpaid homemaking, a job that you don't enjoy obviously has a huge impact on how you feel about your life.

But now that you have that extra brain space to devote to thinking about it, you may discover a way somehow to make your work more interesting. Maybe this is the time to get serious about focusing your energy on your job, then ask for a promotion. Or is this your chance to move on to another employer who would be more appreciative of your brilliance, or to try freelance work in your field? Should you totally re-evaluate your career choice, maybe shift gears completely and go back to school – or decide to stay home? You have talents and skills and now, finally, you'll have a much better chance of figuring out your options because you're not always preoccupied with coping with the clutter and disorganization that surrounded you at home.

But probably the most significant re-thinking task you can take on is re-thinking you. You're no longer weighed down by the responsibility of owning tons of excess stuff or the nagging feeling that you need to deal with it. You can use all of the time, energy and brain space that you previously devoted to buying and cleaning and worrying about stuff to figuring out who you are and what's right for you in your great, new, fabulously unburdened state.

Your hard work has allowed you to redefine your daily routine, certainly noticeably, probably radically. If you continue to apply yourself to this new task with the same kind of determination, you can redefine your entire life in ways that are just as significant.

Travel more, get out and jog, take up needlework – whatever interests you, you now have more time and probably more money to enjoy. Changing jobs, changing locations, changing absolutely nothing except your level of commitment to the choices that you've already made become legitimate possibilities when you're not burdened with truckloads of things.

Try imagining what choices you would make if you were completely stuff-free. Think back to the days when everything you owned could fit in the back of your car. Be as outrageous and as specific as you can. This is your chance to get creative and have some fun without imposing limitations on your ideas.

Then, if you have a spouse, partner or family who will be a part of your future, bring them into a conversation about all the options that you have now that you're un-stuffed. All kinds of interesting possibilities come up when un-stuffed people think about life changes together.

You'll need to be just as diligent at this process of sorting out your life as you were when you were sorting out all that stuff that formerly crowded your home and your head. You'll need to be just as kind to yourself, too, maybe even more so, especially if the fantasy life you envision seems to be pretty far removed from your current reality. Don't worry. Just remember that we already have proof that if we persevere, we can move mountains – literally!

Unloading your unnecessary old stuff was great, but unloading the obligation to continue to be the "old you" gives you the greatest freedom of all.

* * * * *

"Before we set our hearts too much upon anything, let us examine how happy those are who already possess it."

Francois de La Rochefoucauld
1613-1680

MY STORY: THE END OF THE BEGINNING

It's hard to believe that it's been a few years since the fateful night that Darlene and I made our mutual vow to take control of our over-stuffed situations. After she left, we made it a point to stay in contact regularly. We faithfully gave each other much needed encouragement as we fought the good fight against the remarkable quantity of stuff that nearly engulfed our respective homes.

Whenever the sheer volume of things seemed unconquerable and those nasty symptoms of a Stuff Attack cropped up, it was always a great help to have someone to talk to who had not only sympathy but also a bit of perspective to offer at that crucial moment. We rejoiced in our small triumphs (my linen closet is immaculate; her basement holds seasonal clothing in neatly stacked plastic bins); we endured similar woes (gremlins were forever messing up both of our home offices). In time, and with major efforts, we both made admirable progress in eliminating the unnecessary things in our homes and our lives.

Now, on a good day, when I look around the house I'm thrilled to see a distinct difference from that bygone era when the place seemed positively claustrophobic. There's a bit of empty space here, some room to move there. Even my exceptionally shipshape mother thinks it's looking fairly well pulled together. The change gives me quite a wonderful feeling, sort of relaxing and exhilarating all at once.

Occasionally I get a small pang of nostalgia for some of my family things that I passed along in my "pre-estate sale," but ultimately I always conclude that my decisions were correct. Most of the time, I'm content. Sometimes I just sit quietly and reflect, perhaps with a slight bit of wisdom, on the various challenges of disposing of all that stuff.

On a not-so-good day, the work that still needs to be done looms before me like an enormous Himalayan peak. I can acknowledge that there's not nearly as much stuff around but what is left seems, to my chagrin, even more annoying than it had been when it was part of the general melange. I see each thing clearly, in my mind if not out in the open, and it utterly torments me. It's as if I have a stuff allergy. It gives me headaches; it causes crankiness and fatigue. I want to get it out of the house fast! But, of course, I can't, because what's left is some of the most difficult stuff to let go.

There are no huge pieces of extra furniture crowding every inch of livable space and no hidden, mysterious boxes in storage, full of who knows what kinds of things. But it's the itsy, bitsy stuff that remains that drives me crazy. A box of collectibles sits in the hall closet while I attempt to figure out the best way to dispose of each item, a classic example of the Full Value Trap. A selection of old jewelry is stashed away upstairs in a dresser drawer, held hostage by the Sentimental Trap. Too often magazines and papers gather in small piles as they await their release from the curse of Good Intentions. And that's just the beginning. Will I ever get this place totally under control? Will I ever find some peace?!

Well, fortunately the good days occur more frequently and are much closer to reality than the not-so-good days. Un-stuffing is not an easy job and it's not a job with a definitive end in sight. I know that more and more stuff will keep coming into my life every day, so all I can do is work to keep it from swamping me again. But that isn't so bad. The worst is over. The original gigantic mass has been subdued, so creating order becomes a less daunting task.

In fact, when I'm thinking clearly, I realize that it's a life-long process. At times, it might even be called sort of enjoyable (except for that filing part, of course). There is a certain pleasure to be found in the ripping up and shredding of junk mail. I get a tiny bit of a kick when the rice cooker is easily accessible without having to empty an entire kitchen cabinet. And it is rather comforting to know that the checkbooks are safely stowed in the Debit Dossier rather than lost in a sea of confusion. Yes, there is more to do, but I'll get to it. I'll get to it in good time.

For now, I try my best to be a little more comfortable with the lack of perfection that still exists in the house. I try to be a little more forgiving of the lack of perfection in myself, too. When my art supplies seem to creep out of their designated area as if they had little prankster brains guiding them to all corners of the dining room and kitchen, I don't become distraught. I know that it doesn't mean that I've totally lost my grip on keeping things together or that somehow I've failed personally. It just means that I'm busy living my life. When I don't get around to sorting the mail as quickly as I had planned or the kitchen countertop gets a bit cluttered, I don't sink into despair or berate myself for falling behind. I just try to take care of things as soon as I can. I know that it will all work out eventually.

The cleared out brain space has been helpful, too. I think I have more creative ideas for making art. I'm getting a little better at meditating regularly, especially since I now have a good spot to do it without being surrounded by piles of papers. The Writer and I can discuss the possibility of moving again someday without provoking a panic attack at the thought of packing. Overall, I just feel . . . lighter.

* * * * *

Recently I got an excited call from Darlene. She was zooming through town next week on a quick trip and couldn't wait to come by for a visit. Of course, I was delighted that at last I would be able to spend some face-to-face time with her again. But I was also surprised that I felt some anxiety about her seeing the house, even though it was usually in a quite reasonably acceptable state. I made my traditional cup of relaxing chamomile tea, but it wasn't much help. I decided to call Madelaine in the hope that she might soothe my slightly unsettled psyche.

"So, what's the problem? Is the market out of Double Chocolate Mocha Madness?" Maddy asked when I told her the news. In the background I heard sporadic clatter on her computer keyboard and Aretha wailing a familiar refrain from the sixties.

"Nothing that horrible," I laughed, though I shuddered slightly at the thought of such a tragedy. "Actually, I don't really know what's wrong. I think that maybe even after all this time and all that hard work, I'm still feeling just a little insecure about the whole stuff issue."

"But Darlene's been great about supporting you. And you've helped her out, too, right?" Maddy observed, still typing away.

I remained hesitant. "Well, yes, but sometimes it seems like there's so much left that's unfinished . . . "

"Oh, don't be so hard on yourself. Look, what were you doing last night when I called?" she asked.

"Ummm . . . I was ironing my white shirt," I remembered.

"See? You've got nothing to worry about," Maddy announced triumphantly.

I had to think about it for a split second, but then I knew exactly what she meant. The ironing board. It finally had a permanent home in the upstairs closet, never to be misplaced again. I smiled as I realized how bizarre it was that an ironing board had become the very odd symbol of my mostly successful un-stuffing and organizing efforts.

"Of course! You're right," I replied, feeling both relieved and a bit ridiculous. "Thank you, Maddy. It's really sort of embarra . . ."

"Uh-oh. Gotta go. Boss gone berserk," she whispered and quickly signed off. Well, I guess some things never change.

I glanced around and noticed that several days worth of newspapers had piled up on a chair. A half-finished drawing surrounded by colored pencils lay on the dining table. On the floor in front of the bookcase was a stack of books belonging to the Writer that were, as he described it, "in transition." A few other items were scattered about, also wavering on hold while I tried to figure out what to do with them. I knew it would take a little while to straighten up the place.

I leaned back on the sofa and sipped my tea. Everything was just fine.

* * * * *

* * * * *

FINAL TIDBIT: DO IT!

"When all is said and done, more is said than done."

Dorothy Parker

* * * * *

Be the exception to the rule!
Don't just talk about getting rid of stuff. Do it!

* * * * *

Sorting It Out

INDEX OF *TIDBITS*

INDEX OF *TRUE CONFESSIONS*

Sorting It Out

ABOUT THE AUTHOR

Cynthia Friedlob has been a scriptwriter and story editor for numerous children's television shows and family feature films. Her award-winning artwork has been exhibited in gallery and museum shows across the country. Cynthia is a graduate of the University of Denver with both B.A. and M.A. degrees. She lives in the Los Angeles area where she continues to write and make art. She is relatively organized.

Please visit www.CynthiaFriedlob.com to learn more.

Made in the USA
Lexington, KY
27 November 2010